A Badly Painted Picture

Marlon Horton
10th Ward Buck

I'JALE™
PUBLISHING CO.

2019

A Badly Painted Picture

A Badly Painted Picture

Marlon Horton

10th Ward Buck

I'JALE™
PUBLISHING CO.

2019

Copyrights

First Printing: 2019

ISBN 978-0-578-21989-9

I'Jale Publishing Co LLC
2431 Manhattan Blvd
Suite C
Harvey, La. 70058
www.ijalepublishing.com

Table of Contents

A BADLY PAINTED PICTURE

Chapter 1: Rumors Buck

I'm 10th Ward Buck Born Marlon Justin Horton. On the date of September 19, 1980, to the parents of Dawn Horton and Mervin
Riley. I'm the third child of 6.

In order of birth there's Makitha Horton, Mervin Riley Jr., Marlon Horton Sr., Margie Horton, Makivia Horton and Marquel Horton. 3 boys and 3 girls. We were all born and raised in the St. Thomas project.

The St. Thomas project is located Uptown in New Orleans and was considered the most dangerous housing developments in New Orleans. Drugs, crime, and sex. You name it, I've witnessed it all! Seeing those things in real life made it hard for me to watch it on tv because I knew it was fake after seeing real situations play out in front of me. I wasn't the child that would be out because I was afraid of the living.

I hated walking to and from school, I hated attending events and I even hated going to the store. As I got older in my youth years, I started to adjust by hanging with relatives and going by my cousins' house. My cousins were more exposed to the community so I would pick up little survival tips from them. Basically, mind your own business, ask no questions and even if you did see something, you did not see anything.

Knowing this made it easier for me to go out and be a part of the population. This was something I needed because the only place I would see friends was at school. No phones, no social media or nothing so it was school and then home for me. I didn't find being inside unusual because I was used to it. I would be inside trying to take apart gadgets and things trying to invent other things.

Me and my oldest brother had bunk beds. He had the bottom and I had the top. Under my matters was my chest, which was my storage area where I kept all kinds of crap. If you raise my mattress up, you would find all kinds of things from batteries to wires and all kinds of tools. After I completed my homework this was how I kept myself busy.

I wasn't a nerd, but I was damn close. At age 7, my momma
enrolled me in a place called Kingsley House. Kingsley House is a facility that had daycare services for toddlers, elderly adults, and after school program for the youth.

Kingsley House was awesome I mean awesome! It's where me and my friend Flo and others would meet after school and have a blast. During school time we would attend Kingsley's house after and for the summer attend its summer camp. Kingsley House had it going on! Filed trips, sporting events outings, swimming, cooking gosh you name it and Kingsley house had us apart of it.

Kingsley house gave us an outlook on life and helped us explore different opportunities. The heart of Kingsley House for me was the connection I had with friends from the other side of my project.

There was the Eastside which was Flo side and the Southside which was my side, and there use to be this neighborhood beef between the two sides. I never understood it but once we were at Kingsley House, we were together. This is where the pictures of me started to be painted badly.

I love to compete, and I was at the top when it came to competition. Racing and swimming were both my number ones. With that, came hate and dislike cause when people wanted to join my circle, I wouldn't let them because I didn't want what they had going on to affect me. For example; if a certain person was in beef, I didn't want that person that they're beefing with to throw me in it.

Well, the mess found its way to me anyway. The other guys who I didn't want to hang with would tell my friends that I don't mean them no good and when I win, I don't give them any credit, or they say I only talk about me when I win. They were basically making it as if I was telling them some things when I never even communicated with them. However, it was hard for me to convince my friends because once Kingsley house was over, we didn't see each other again until the next day after school.

Now they don't take no time at all talking and telling lies about me. All this just to be in my company. Rumors have been here before us and will be here when we are long gone. What's amazing is that people would believe a rumor about others before checking for the facts. That's crazy because it's not like they didn't hear rumors about themselves before. People are quick to judge and assume over something they heard. Talking about a person and spreading lies about them is low and dangerous and I've been dealing with this forever.

I'm not gay and have nothing against gays. I have a gay cousin in which our family was tight, so we embraced him and his friends. The fact that I'll be with him or have conversations with his friends' people would look down on that and remember back then this was unusual for a straight male to be around that as often as I was, but it was a family thing that turned business for me because I discovered a group called SWA.

SWA included my cousin and his friends. They were a bounce rap group. As far as me being gay, I'm not! The rumors started to pick up wind with the signing of this group. It wasn't bad because those that hung with me knew what was up. It was only those against me that would say that to be mean or distract others from being around me. I hate bringing this up because it's a FLAT-OUT LIE!

I never, ever had sex with my cousin but I would admit as a child, I remember we both were watching tv and I said something about a woman and he goes "boy you got a small thing you can't do nothing with that woman" and I responded by saying , "boy I got her" and somewhere he convinced me to show him my penis.

I didn't think nothing of it, but as I got to know him, I realized he manipulated me to see my private part. To me it was a small deal, so I never brought it up are addressed it because it was a Penny on a dollar compared to some of the other stories of him and little boys. Lowering boys in with conversation, food and money. Remember even though I see it, I didn't see it.

It's crazy because the little boys that would engage with him acted totally innocent and wasn't getting the gay charge, but here go me getting the charges for everything. Sometimes it seemed as though something goes wrong with or for someone it becomes the blame factor.

As stated, I have nothing against gays however, I don't want that bad low on my name. I know it was false and was used to make me look bad, but my concern was the females. I didn't want them to think I was gay.

Speaking on the females, some of them were having sex with boys that were having sex with the gay men and a few of them were in relationships, still I minded my business. Still to this day, there are females messing with dudes who secretly mess with dudes but hey she like who she likes. Some are in love leading to fighting over a dude.

Back then I saw woman fight men over men and to this day it's still happening. It's one thing to hear about these things but mind bothering when you become a witness. All this craziness happens, and it gets swept under the rug. But when it's about Buck and false it gets stretched and blown out of context. At first, I never understood the importance of mentioning me but now I see with the attention I get, people think for them to get on or noticed, they must say Buck name.

10th Ward Buck

I never start with people but when I respond to their BS by defending myself people blame me as the aggressor. Far too long this have been going on where people pick with me by saying something or posting trying to get my attention. Even if I block them off my social media platforms they still reach. As much as I try to ignore it, I still just go off speaking on the lies.

My life is just that and people seem to want me to act a certain way but I'm human as well. A person can only take so much! It would start out as dislike because they don't like the way I address things pertaining to my life. After the dislike comes hate. They would comment on my post and live, then turn around and get mad when I block them. Once they play, they become angry and any bad thing said about me they would dip in it and start more shit. It's a pack of hating ass people who are formulated from my block list. Now that the dislike and hate don't work the lies start.

One local artist has this down pack as 75 to 85 percent of his conversation is about me. Buck this and Buck that with all the false info. This same dude I employed and gave him shows. This is a perfect example about watching your enemy, sometimes they can be the people in your company or who you are doing business with. He knows nothing personal about me nothing! All his info is false, and his goal is to make me look bad.

Him as well as others feels that the only way to take me down is to bash me, but 10 years later this same shit is happening and I'm still here entertaining! We both do bounce music and it's not a competition but for some reason he is just like others.

For some reason, bounce artist thinks just because we do the same music that we have to compete. New Orleans have that crabs in the barrel mentality when it comes to business of any sort. No matter the field there's always some people somewhere in this beefing about their product and Bounce music is no different. We beef amongst each other, write music and talk about each other instead of us coming together. Everybody wants to be the best, but more than 50 percent don't even have a reputable song catalog. How dare you put yourself up there with legends just to get attention. It's nothing wrong with thinking you the best but come on now, some of you all be looking for trouble.

What I get out of saying you the best is that you are throwing shots at those of us with history and hit songs already in the streets. Lately, that act has been causing Feud between the Bounce artist and they've been going back and forward on the internet but not producing music. There were several unknown artist taking shots at me, but I ignored, and they fell off. When it comes to entertaining that mess, I dodge it. That's something I do not want to be a part of because I'm all about unity.

When it comes to bounce unity, I lead the way as not only do I give events and employ my fellow artist, I even tried to give a bounce show called "Bounce Summit" where we all come together and make money. Just like everything else that event fell apart, although the event still happened, it fell apart because of the lack of participation from others.

There was a lack of unity because after the first few meetings a certain DJ went to talking crazy to the artist saying Buck going to get paid the most. Any chance he had to kill the event he did! He attended the meetings but wanted control, y'all know when I'm using my brains no one can control that situation. The Bounce summit was the perfect way and start to us as of fellow artist to coming together as 1. There were guest speakers, special talents and Bounce artist. People always want control instead of getting a role in the functions and playing your part. I paid all expenses for all the artist along with their pay, but before the hatred got to the artist and made them suspicious about the event. It's amazing how people can be so easily influenced. Therefore, we can't come together because everybody wants to be the teacher but not 1 student listen!

People need to start listening. Everybody wants things to go their way instead of coming together and pitch in ideas making it easier for things to happen. Team work makes the dream work. So, use my portion of this, yours of this, his of that and her little idea. Now we all have input and we all have our little ideas in motion, so now we see things a little clearer.

As much as I love my city it's the people that fucks things up. I'm a firm believer in unity no matter race, gender or sexuality. We all are Gods' children so we shouldn't dislike one another or beef over things that can be resolved with a little conversation. I'm often looked down on cause I'm quick to defuse a situation. They like to call me a peace maker. It's best to get to the bottom of a problem than to keep it going over a simple misunderstanding.

Although with most problems more than 75% of the problems and beef in my city stems from little things. He says, she says, stepping on somebody shoe, when you look at a person, they said something about my momma etc. just flat out petty.

Most of the big beef stems from old beef from back in the day, this Ward against that Ward, retaliation from another murder, tried to rob or jack somebody, he tried to holla at my girl or trying to hustle on the same block. Bruh, all this is sickening!

After all these years of the same bullshit, nobody has the sense to see that it always ends with a death or a jail sentence. Before you know it then it's beef and people can't really go nowhere. They spoked and looking over their shoulders 24/7 because they are thinking their enemy is everywhere. I rolled a few times or ran into some dudes that had beef and each time the conversation was kind of scary.

As we talk, they are looking loaded and watching the surrounding like a security guard. Nobody should have to live like that and us innocent people shouldn't be caught up in that. So many innocent lives are taken because the main target never gets hit. From run ups to drive by shootings, when these dudes shoot, they don't aim they spray.

10th Ward Buck

When I say spray, they shoot at everybody and everything on the block including kids, animals, houses and cars. In my head I'm like wow, do they even care about the kids! I mean come on, let the babies live. This makes it harder to raise your children in certain communities. They can't go outside, you can't send them to the store I mean all the things that goes with growing up is taken away.

Years ago, at the Muses parade my cousin was killed. She was an innocent by stander who was hit with a bullet when 2 guys saw the person they were beefing with and shot in to a crowd of people. I was right there as I ran when I heard the shots being fired and fell scraping my hands and knees not knowing she was hit.

As the scene cleared, I found out it was her. Our family went to the hospital where they told us she passed away. She was taken away from us! Her family, her mother, brothers and sister and was more devastating than her son. Pain runs deep and to see a child look for their mother is heartbreaking then to see a mother seeing her child in a coffin from stupidity is awful! It took a toll on my family and it also ruined our Mardi Gras experience. My family is strong though as we come together each year on that same parade day and release balloons in remembrance of her.

These guys are not only taking away people from this earth they are also affecting others livelihood. I will not say that they don't understand the pain because they have lost relatives or friends too. At some point these young men must be encouraged that this isn't what's up.

See, society, music and movies have these young men thinking this is what's up. They live for credit and brag on the murders. My solution would be for these females to cut them off and not deal with them. Do not give them boys no hug, kiss, conversation or sex. Most of the times all they do is looking to not only impress girls but intimidate others. No gun and they're as humble as can be. They get caught they cry, they get time they cry and rat but if they're free they want to be this iron chest Charlie that without a gun they're not. They are more like Charlene. For years people have been trying to put in solutions for murders, but history just keeps repeating itself with different people.

Respect starts in the home however we can't blame it on parents all the time. Once a child goes out the house who he or she choose to hang out with determines how they live their lives. Children should want to do right for themselves to endure they'll have a good future. When we blame others and not those at fault it makes those at fault feel they can get away with things more.

Example, there are some dudes who either shot someone or committed robbery and got off on the charges and went right back and did those same things. When you think you can get away with something you do it especially if your charges were dropped. That's just the ones who were caught just imagine those that didn't get caught they will continue their criminal ways. This is all because from jump they were not getting the blame like they should. We need to find a solution and stop blaming parents because people will do what they want regardless.

10th Ward Buck

We all know it's a fact that once we walk out of our parents' house, we are free to do what we want. We all have done things we shouldn't and continued as long as we didn't get caught, well that's the same mindset of a criminal. But here is the big boom, you have some that gets caught all the time, but the system keeps letting them off the hook.

These are the dangerous ones because they know or have it in their head that I am going to get caught, do a little time and come back home. They have the whole system down like a school project. The parents need assistance from the community. The best solution can be the people they hang out with.

A real friend will tell you the real and be like this isn't what's up, we must change for our future. We get old not young and we can't do this our whole lives. I can't and will not hang with a person if I can't change their bad habits that will affect our lively hood. When the world sees my friend or friends, they see me and when they see them, I want them to see positivity. If we were in beef when the enemy wants you but see me, they will attack me for being your friend. Friends are supposed to back one another for the good and not allow them to fall victim to the same BS that have a black eye over our city.

How could a city like New Orleans be so rich in culture from Mardi Gras, 2nd lines, DJ's and the food…. but have bad baggage? This should not be. We as Black people came together back then to free ourselves from slavery to fighting for our freedom and fighting to be in the same places as whites to fighting against each other. We rally and protest when another race of people mocks us or say something about us but when we harm each other it gets swept under the rug. It bothers me bad! It's crazy we come together for certain things and not all things. We must fix this amongst us. We need to stop instigating mess between one another. It's time to get to the bottom of things. Why are you hurting, what's bothering you, how can I help? Just a simple conversation can help. We shy away from talking to people but sometimes it's what they need.

A shoulder to cry on or an ear that will listen. Even with our kids, we must listen to them and stop being so angry with them all the time. My oldest sister and mom help me with this. I expect better from my oldest son and when I hear he did a certain thing I would just go off and not listen and talk calmly.

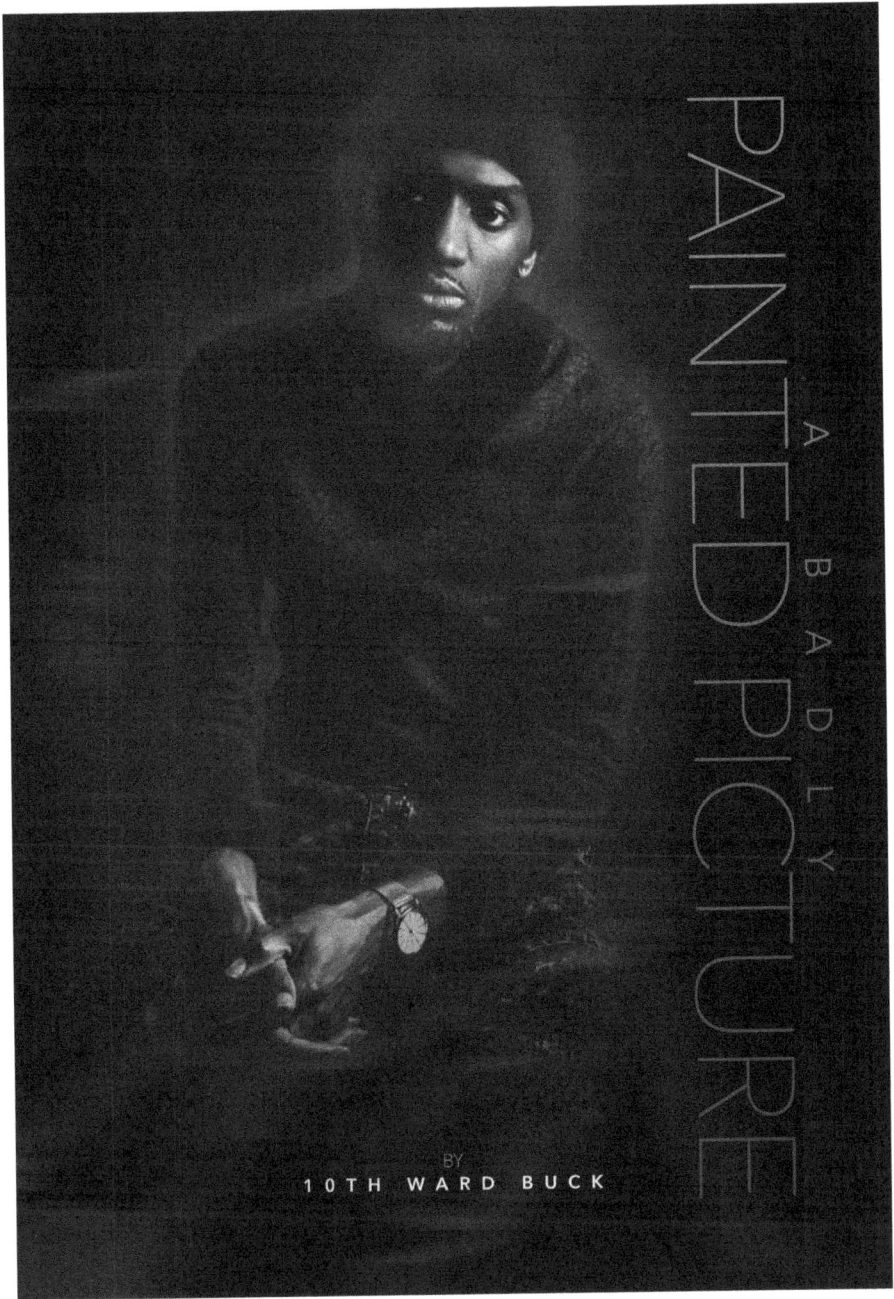

When you attack your kids, they feel as if they don't have nobody else who would defend them so anger and frustration builds up inside of them. I've witnessed this with my son. I had to rethink my situation, hear him out and talk to him more instead... "hello, what you want." I had to make time for him. This is a big problem because we make time for others and give our kids none. These kids didn't ask to come here so we need to step up to the plate and provide. The same way we make time for others we need to make for our kids. If the parents don't influence the kids, then the outside world will!

Chapter 2:

10th Ward Buck

Sporting activities as a child made me popular in my hood. My claim to popularity in New Orleans started in 1995 when I appeared in a movie called "Dead Man Walking." This movie starred Susan Sarandon and Sean Penn. This movie was about a Nun who worked in the St. Thomas project and took on a project being against the death penalty. The movie was filmed in the St. Thomas project and the casting director was looking for children to play different roles. I was introduced to the casting director Ms. Tracy KILPATRICK.

She asked me to help her find kids for the movie and was looking for 1 young black kid to play the role of Herbie. So, I went out and got a lot of my peers to sign up, but she couldn't find a kid to play Herbie. I then went to my school and found more kids, still no Herbie but then she asked me.

At first, I was like no, knowing that I was offering the opportunity to others. I then went home talk to my mom and she said to go for it. I tried out for the part and got it. Hundreds of kids went for the role but somehow it fit me. I didn't like reading at all. I'm outgoing and like to figure things out with little reading as possible but then boom the casting director gave me a script with lines to read. I was like o my lord! What have I gotten myself into!

So, I'll go home and practice but what made it better me and the agent became friends, so she helped me perfect the lines and taught me the ins and outs of auditioning for movies. Before this movie I struggled with reading and now I understand the concept and can answer after reading.

My thoughts on reading was to just read so that's what I did without taking in the story.

This was a life changing experience for me as my grades in reading became better. A few days later my mom got the contract and it had my pay in bold print. MARLON HORTON TO BE PAID $500 A DAY. Wow, seeing that was so unbelievable. Still to this day I'm getting paid for that movie. I get a residual check every 3 months. A kid my age in the hood getting that amount of money at that time bih, I was hood rich. No matter what my momma needed she made sure I seen every penny. So, I brought a car.

Age 15 my neighbor was on drugs and he sold his 1988 cutlass to me for $800 but I gave him $500. I figured crackheads always come short let me see if my $500 would do it and like a charm the car was mine.

The car was white, so I went to radio shack a brought a small black tv and put it on the dash. Then I brought a light that looked like a police light. Me and my friends would ride up Tchoupitoulas, flash the light in cars in front of us and watch them pull over. They thought we were pulling them over. This was wrong but for our age it was fun. I would drive up, flash the light then look at them, laugh and pull off. We didn't mean no harm but hey our fun is our fun.

I used to drive wildly up and down St. Thomas showing off and this 1 time I gave my car to my barber and he did a 360 in my shit, I was pissed off. I thought things like that would mess my car up but then he taught me, and I became a 360 machine and even learned how to power break. I was dare devil!

My fun ended when this one day I was riding up St. Thomas and when I got to Adele, I did a 360 and at the completion of the turn my bumper was face to face with a child whose father was holding her hand. Whew, close call! The 360 usually completes in a circle in the middle of the streets but the fast speed made me lose control. From that day, I never did a 360, power break or pulled people over. That was a life changing experience. If I would have hit that child maybe, I'll still be in jail today depending what the outcome was. That was my wake-up call. We all get wake up calls.

Different times in different situations but we must read and apply them. I talked to my newly friend Tracy about the incident and she informed me on consequences people she knows are facing, and from that conversation, we became close.

As the movie began to film, I became humble and more informative to others around me about things they're doing and the choices they make. We all have choices we just must choose the right one. Meeting Tracy was great. After the film and we became close. Before she left, she gave me the same camera she used to interview me with. Not sure why or what I'll do with it. I took time learning the camera.

After learning the basics of it my first work was porn. Don't judge me. Me and this girl would have sex and record it then watch it. We discussed our moves and what we were going to do next time.   Its views weren't all that because it was on a stand so I couldn't adjust like it could if I had a camera man.

Looking back, it's funny cause as kids you mimic what you hear and see, and I was one that did that all too often. Me seeing things was the reason I didn't like to read because I figured why waste time reading when I can learn on my own.   As time went on, I was comfortable with leaving the footage in the camera because no one knew how to work it. But one day I got a new set of tapes and took our sex video out, sat it down and to this day not sure what happened to it. I was terrified! I was looking high and low. My heart would stop and start again! Loosing things is one thing but loosing sex footage oh God, take me now!

Whew! I learned my lesson. I had to be more careful. The next project I did was made a movie with my friends and my sister friends in my momma house. I made a little story and we filmed it while my momma was at work. She had things around the house that she didn't want touched but we still moved them out the way to make the movie happen. I was getting my Spike Lee on. I just knew I had it going on. What's crazy is I had a team of people down with me.

Since I just filmed the big movie "Dead Man Walking" the people I had down with me thought I knew what I was talking about. I was just free styling. From there, I was just a camera head. Filming basketball, football you name it my little camera was keeping me busy.

10th Ward Buck

Tracy took me on my first road trip. I went to Alabama before with family, but it was family reasons and ,6 awful hours and I hated it. But here go Tracy taking me on the road to North Carolina. It was 14 hours gosh. So long, when I got there, I didn't want to leave because I was thinking about 14 hours back.

While on the road there was an accident where we witnessed a car tumbling and it rolled over to our side and the car bounced in front of us and went over. Our car was hit heavy with a lot of gravel and strong winds. Close call! One second faster and we were hit. My life flashed before my eyes. It was scary. I got home and to this day never told my momma that story or about the long 14 hours because I enjoyed the trip and didn't want her to feel uncomfortable about my next trip.

Thereafter I got a call from Susan Sarandon who was at the time in a relationship with Tim Robbins. Tim directed Dead Man Walking. Tim, Susan, and I became friends as we talked about life. Where they were and how they get there and how is it for me living in the project. The call was asking to speak with my momma about me flying out to New York to spend a week at their mansion. Here I am in New York 16 years old first class everything. Airport, front of the plane first class things I'll only see in a movie.

When I arrived, I expected to see them, but it was a driver holding a sign with my name on it. The driver escorted me to his car which was a limo. I'm like wow! He took me to their Manhattan home which is this big building with apartments thru out. But they brought out a whole floor, wow it was beautiful. One of their bathrooms consisted of gold bathroom fixtures which held all their awards. A site to see.

So truthfully, at the time I didn't know how famous they were in fact I didn't even know who they were before the movie. We went out in public to an event and there were cameras flashing everywhere and all I remember is Susan putting her coat over my head hiding me from the media. We get in the event and it was all A list actors and actresses. People my momma and my grandma watched on tv. They were clean, well dressed, and groomed. The setting was that of a top-notch wedding or shall I say royal wedding. The food was very well catered. I met so many stars and what was crazy I didn't know their names just faces.

The next day they took me to a hockey game. Now, when they said we was going to a hockey game I thought to myself black people don't go to hockey games. I later found out the Tim loved hockey and even played. I didn't know what to expect going to this game, so I wasn't so hyped about it but boy it was everything and more.

First it was the battle of New York, it was a riviera game. New York Rangers against the New York Islanders the top 2 teams at the time. It was like the Saints vs Falcons or Saints vs Cowboys which are very hyped games. It was packed and sold out. We had low seats right by the team. The game started and it was awesome! The skating, the shots the fighting. I would have never known hockey was that intense and exciting.

10th Ward Buck

After the game we went into the New York Rangers locker room where I was introduced to the team that included Hall of Famer Wayne Gretzky. The whole team autographed a hockey puck and gave it to me.

I played around and didn't cherish it. I remember on the show Pawn Stars I seen an autograph go for $59,000 for one-person autograph. Mine had the whole team autograph and I lost it.

Three days in after eating top foods healthy foods Tim asked me what I want to eat on my last day. I replied Popeyes chicken. So, then we drove from their city home to their other home outside New York City limits. Just when I thought the first house was everything this second house had all the amenities and more. The house was literally on the hill. Looking out the window the pool was below. Bruh, it was lit!

At this house we got to know each other more and did more family like activities. On my last day they called me in the kitchen for dinner and said you remember what you asked for on your last day, I replied yes Popeyes chicken and they said yep and open the oven it was chicken pot pie. Bruh, I was puzzled they were like what. I said what is that they said chicken pot pie, I replied no! Popeyes chicken in which it didn't hit them like it would hit us. They were then puzzled like oooooo. However, I ate the chicken pot pie and now it's my favorite dish from KFC I love in now. Got back home and even though our house was clean I still felt it was dirty.

The movie comes out reach the top and Susan wins Oscar for best actress. The release of the movie blew me up more in the project. Next phone call comes from Sister Helen who is the writer of the book Dead Man Walking. She was chosen to run with the Olympic Torch in 1996 and asked me to run with her. It was beautiful, there were crowds of people waiting for the torch to get to us as we ran a few blocks to light the next persons.

After our run, Sister Helen let me keep the torch but just like the hockey puck and other awards I didn't take care of it. I've had all kinds of souvenirs and didn't take care of them. Tracy worked with Martin Lawrence and got a leather jacket from his Martin show and gave it to me. Ask me where it is at?

I went to a Jay Z concert where while on stage he autographs a hat and threw it in the crowd. I saw people just jumping around but the signed New York hat landed in my arms. Ask me where it's at.

Looking back even if I would have auctioned those items off, I'll be better off.

After a year, Tracy returned to New Orleans putting me in more movies. She introduced me to bowling and I fell in love with it. She kept me grounded and would always say take care of your mamma. As busy as she was, she found time to communicate with me. When you are around the right people you receive the right things. I'm grateful to have met her. Not only was I learning from her I was able to teach others what I've learned and witnessed.

A few months later Tim asked me about pursuing a career in acting. I enrolled in NOCCA and they paid my tuition. They were serious about my future. I would preach and preach that I stay focused in school and not get distracted by anything.

My first year in high school, I was short and joined the band. They called me Tea-Cup. The upper-class member loved to tease me and ask me to sing my song "I'm a little tea pot". No matter we were, they would ask me to sing.

Because of my popularity I didn't get teased as much as others, but I do remember 1 time where the bass drummer took the drum stick and him me in my forehead. It didn't hurt, it was more of my feelings being hurt. I had to much pride and felt like that should have not happened, but it did, and I cried. My feelings were hurt.

That lil lick wasn't nothing compared to my friends being punched and kicked not too hard, but it was there.

Overall, I enjoyed the band my freshmen year. Although I was small, I was good in football and I was fast. I went to practice a few times and received my helmet, but that band jacket meant too much to me to not get. When I used to go to football practice then band class Mr. Brimmer, the band director would say those of you on the football team will not get a jacket.

I was like wow I must decide. The fact that the other guys on the football team were way bigger than me I choose to stay in the band full time but just like everything else I'm not sure where my band jackets is.

In middle school and before the movie I played boyfriend girlfriend with my girlfriend Re Re who is 2 months older than me. Now high school and stardom I got away from being with her. Nothing intentionally but I just didn't have as much time as before.

When you are in a relationship you must put in time and when you don't you lose those people. I rather her move on than for me to waste her time. I didn't go to being a dog or anything. Then and now I'm a firm believer you should not waste a person's time. It's hard to love with little time spent. I'm for love, far too often I see people fake relationships, I can't I'm too real for that.

With the right people in your corner your life is set up for success. At times we shy away from opening ourselves up to people. It's something about our pride which holds us back. This time I went for it and I won.

I've opened up to Tracy and anybody who wanted information. I found that talking about your problems relieves some of the pressure. I remember one time having a conversation with my mother and I was crying, and she made a statement she said, "son you are no different" and from there I instantly stopped crying. It made since because I was stuck up on cloud 9 expecting certain things not to happen to me but her statement made me realize that the rules of life apply to me also. And that's why when people bother me about certain things I do, I dust it off cause the

10th Ward Buck

have to realize I'm human to. I make wrong decisions and mistakes Just like y'all.

I think was people realize I'm capable of making mistakes as well the dislike for me would fade. Right now, they expect too much from me. I'm not that person they make me out to be. Because of the heart I have to help others I have been taken advantage of. I'm here to help but with so many biting the hand that feeds them it becomes harder to help the next person. Even though it becomes hard and I have my doubts, I still help as much as I can

. I can't let what has happened in the past stop me for helping someone else. At this point I take it as my calling. I've helped so many from school enrollment, to music to business and most of the time they get where they want to go and do not acknowledge me, but I don't get upset because as I stated it's my calling.

For me to stay relevant I know I have to put others on and that's why I do it. Sometimes it ends up being the wrong people, but you never know who's up to what in the beginning. I've put so many on and have been bitten more than 50 percent of the time and that's because once I start to help someone and then stop, they get mad and feel I'm abandoning them, but I only can get them so far.

So, once I reach that level I back up and let them control their own ship. Most of the time they are lazy and fail to realize that they have to learn as we go. When I do part ways, they can handle their own business. I never just stop communication between me and others, I just stop helping as much as I was in the beginning.

As seen on my social media sites, those who were with me before taking to social and blast me to make them look good and never admit the truth. The steps are always the same. Dislike, hatred then lies.

I never understood how people can be for you if you are helping, but the moment you get to doing you, it's a problem. The truth about everybody I've been around was them rushing to the spotlight. I always explain to my crew we all can't be headliners. I always say just play your role and your time will come. I never knew the level of respect they had for me would drop low. I mean bashing and even joining the enemy. I swallowed that pill of betrayal because I figured if they go on that side it's where they always wanted to be.

When a person shows you who they are believe them. When a person wants to leave let them. It's better to distance yourself from those who don't want to be around you then to have them pretend they're happy with you. It was a tough lesson for me, and I had to learn the hard way. There were signs everywhere each time but, I didn't read them.

Looking back, I see them all. I'm not going to stop being there but I'm not going to be a fool anymore either. It's bad when former members of your camp turn on you and tell lies because people think the lies are true because those people ran with you. I never fucked over no one in my click. If they needed anything I was there. Whenever

10ᵗʰ Ward Buck

something went down, I was first on their list to call. So, this bullshit they pulled off and the lies wasn't caused for. As friends we should have met, talked about the problem or problems and hashed it out among us. People be quick to run to the internet with bullshit but fail to realize they going to run in to me again.

A Badly Painted Picture

Chapter 3:

Music wasn't on my list. It was a thing for my oldest brother Melvin known as Merv Swerv, RIP. He would write and write and make hooks all day long. He would always tell me I should try it, but it was out of my league.

One day me and my friend Big Keith, RIP as well. Was walking around the project and he told a girl to get her drawls out her booty. Then instantly, I repeated it and started to rap it. Later, I added more words then it became a song.

I would see different girls outside and say their name followed by get your drawls out your booty say what get your drawls out your booty. The hood loved it!

Then one day there was a big DJ in the project where DJ Jubilee was the DJ at a party, and somebody told him I wanted to rap. I didn't want to rap but hey Jubilee called me up and this is how I got my stage name 10th Ward Buck. Jubilee grab the mic and said y'all welcome to the stage 10th Ward Buck. Me and my friends got on the stage and rock the crowd. Everybody wanted their name to be called. It was a hit!

From there, I would go to the studio and back DJ Jubilee. If you listen to most of his songs, you'll hear us in the background yelling school names, wards etc. Jubilee would get a van and load 20 to 30 of us and bring us to the studio to hype his music. This was the first time I seen a studio. On one of my visits to the studio I exchanged info with the studio's owner engineer. I started hanging around Take Fo Records, going to studio sessions, meetings and concerts.   One show at the House of Blues, I was too young to get in, so I had to be in a Mario suit. At the time jubilee just dropped the song "Do the Mario."

Day by day event by event, I was learning as much as I could about the music business.   Not all events were peaches and cream.

One event a big fight broke out that started inside and escalated outside. People were running everywhere then suddenly I felt a punch that knocked me into today because I still feel it.! Right after he hit me, he looks and said my bad Buck. It was someone from my hood, he thought I was on the other team. When I tell you, nothing hurts worse than a punch you don't see coming. O jeesh, don't want to feel that again. Now, I be very careful going to events.

Although I had a hit song at the time Take Fo Records wasn't ready for me to become an artist. At the time they just released Katey Redd in which it was new and unexpected for them to release a gay artist on their label, but it was a hit. So, their focus was Katey. I would make song after song but still no deal. I then started to call the studio and found out that I can pay for my own studio time.

After going to Take Fo Records with my songs, I went to Katey and told him I had a song called "Shake it like a". He heard it and liked it so I paid for studio time to have it recorded. We recorded the song and it was a hit.

One day I ran into Choppa Chop aka Choppa Style and we wanted to record a song so I told him I have a studio session I have paid for that he can come and record on. Choppa showed up and not only did I pay for his first studio session I created the best to his first song that got him a deal with Take Fo then later singing with no limit record. Music is fun. It's where you can express yourself or help others express themselves. The best part is hearing people sing your music and tell you how much they love it. Going to parties hearing your music, car passing blasting it and people paying you to entertain them and their guess at events. It's a wonderful feeling that can't be explained.

As we were forced to move out the St. Thomas project because it was closed down for a new development, we moved about a mile away to Annunciation St. It felt strange because all I knew was the project. There were no more groups of people outside playing. No more seeing your regular friends and neighbor. No more snack lady it was just us.

One day I went outside and heard music coming from across the street from my house day after day. I then saw this black dude with a small Afro on his head and asked him if he knew where that music was coming from and he said yes "me" I was like Yey, he said yep. We exchanged numbers and became friends. The dude_was BlaqNmild. He had beats for days. To an artist he was God. He had and was everything an artist needed and wanted. Beats and a place to record. Blaq and I started making these mix bounce cd and it was a hit. Selling in our neighborhood and selling out at Fortier basketball games. We put out about 4 mix bounce R & B CDs then he started working on his BlaqNmild mix volume CDs.

We then met and became friends with Roca B who lived on our block as well. Roca B was known for singing and selling CDs. We found out he sung and asked him to sing live over a track and then boom Roca B was introduced to the Bounce community.

Later I introduced Peacachoo to Blaq and Peacachoo learned the way Blaq recorded. The acid program got to others because of Peacachoo as he strated to teach it to others.

Many nights in the mix of us working, I would fall asleep by Blaq then 1 day in my sleep I kept hearing this fast beat. It was Peacachoo on the computer playing it and I started saying Fasta Fasta Fasta and boom it was the hottest song in the city and number 1 on Q93 for months.

At one of my events I met Lucky Johnson. He introduced himself followed by whom I am signed to. We exchanged numbers and later I hooked up with him joining his label Biggface records. Biggface had a bunch of dancers but not a for sure bounce artists. There were straight and gay male dancers so Lucky split them by giving me the straight dancers who became the Fasta Boys. This created the boy group dance team craze and bounce battle. The Fasta Boys were the hottest dance group out. I made posters with their pictures on it and the girls took them down as fast as they went up. We were killing shows.

Later the Fasta Boys recorded their own hit song "I ain't have sex in a long time". We were the Jackson 5 of bounce. We were at every middle and high school functions. No matter where you went you heard us. It's funny because people would be out of breath trying to keep up with the tempo of the song. This song influenced the tempo and why Bounce is faster than before. When we dropped this song, we didn't think it would have this effect. Both radio stations were playing the song. We were doing interviews and radio drops.

After the wave of Fasta, was my next song Drop and give me 50. This song was unique as this song started the way songs are being made and chopped up as Drop and give me 50 was the first song chopped up using one word to carry a song. The song was so hot it was later purchased from me and Blaqnmild by Warner Brother records for Mike Jones and Hurricane Chris. My song went worldwide.

When I first received the call from Mike Jones, he was the hottest artist at the time so him calling me about my song was exciting. We started talking then he let me hear the song. When I heard it, I knew right then it was going to be a hit. We then met up with the label and we signed the song over. We were invited to the video shoot, it was a blessing and humbling experience. I mean our work went further than New Orleans.

This song started the fall out between me and Blaq as people would tell him I got more than him, but he was there when I signed the contract. There was one check that came to my house for $56,000 which was supposed to be split between me, Blaq, Hurricane Chris and Mike Jones. Once the label found out, they canceled the check. I couldn't cash it when I got it on the weekend, and it was from Bank of America in which there isn't a branch here in New Orleans.

Blaq and I remained cool but as time went on, he distant himself away from me. Some of the same things we talked about doing for each other when he got on, he didn't do them. He did work with Master P and never invited me to Cali or to any events and when he did the Drake songs. He did call me to tell me he was working with him, but when I asked him to let me know when they were filming, he didn't.

My last cd project I reaches out to him for a song or 2 and he said let's do it but never returned my calls or messages. All this stemmed from what he was told years ago about me getting more money off our "Drop and Give me 50" record deal. I don't even know how people figured that out. Then come to find out, it all began because of a lie.

This started to become too often in my life as others want to be a part of it so bad that if I don't allow them, they go to people in my crew and start crap with them.

However, we continued to make music together. We were a runner up in the 2014 NOLA awards.

Then I recorded Where is d boys which started as a joke. I was acting as Beesha and made a statement about the dude I was teasing I said, "where is d boys" and that became a hit with Instagram and Facebook. People would ask me to say that line over and over. They got a kick out of it. So, I said let me make a song and I done so. It was the city's new anthem.

In 2014 it won a NOLA award for hottest song of the year. The last song me and Blaq did end up being a hit as well, Fifty 5. Boy this song was and still is everything. It led me to winning hottest bounce artist in 2015. Thereafter I went on a drought from doing music, as Blaq started working with Master P more often. I wasn't used to recording with others, so I didn't try.

It was the chemistry we created that I was used to. The conversation, the jokes etc. I can go to the studio a whole day and not record one song, but still leave with some knowledge of some sort or just catch up on time. We talked for hours about our future and what we wanted, where we should be and more goals.

The bond was there. That bond allowed us to be there for each other and when it came to music, we trusted each other. Every song I recorded with Blaq ended up a different way when he finished it. I would record "shake it, bounce it do it" and when I get it from Blaq it would be like " sha sha sha shake it, shake it shakie it shake it, bounce it do it bounce it bounce it" you know adding and changing things around.

That's what I loved about working with Blaq. Once I record, he took it from there. He would not call and ask for the order he was just create his own. Blaq is really a musical genius. After putting out so many hit records the whole city wanted that BlaqNmilD sound. At first, he was going by his real name Adam then we got to a point when we was like bruh you need a producer name so we threw out names and then he said Blaqnmild and at the time it sounded crazy to me, so I was like no be he insisted so boom Blaqnmild was born. On the other hand, that was this DJ named DJ Blaqnmild and boy that caused a lil beef.

For my producer Blaq, he wasn't receiving the credit he worked for because he wasn't well known. He didn't go out or anything to show his face, but Dj Blaqnmild was out in the streets so boom he got all the credit for work my friend Blaq was doing. They passed words several times. Dj Blaqnmild would say that the producer wants to be like him and my Blaqnmild would throw_shots over beats to the DJ. Boy it was a time and something unexpected.

Meanwhile I was talking to Blaqnmild and said see that's why I said don't go with that name and jokily Blaq said fuck that boy. So, it was fuck him and on we went about our business. I didn't have no beef with DJ Blaqnmild at all. As time went on the beef between them to disappeared.

Years later, even though we didn't do another full song together. I then recorded a commercial for a well know Attorney from New Orleans with Blaqnmild. I told Blaqnmild I had this idea and wanted to pitch it to the attorney. So, he recorded it. I never discussed how much I spent to do the idea. I had to pay the camera crew, the dance team, T-shirt's and the dancers. I didn't think Blaqnmild would have asked to be paid, I considered him as a friend and I never paid him because we worked together and we both benefited. Whenever he needed something I was there or when I made a lil extra from somewhere I took care of him however the money wasn't plentiful at the time.

So, I pitched the idea and it didn't get excepted till 2 years later. When it did, it went on tv and radio then Blaqnmild told me I never paid him for the song. I was shocked cause he never asked me that before. Here's the truth though, the deal was set up in stages.

The next payment was the profit payment, but it all happened_so quickly I didn't have time to piece all of the puzzle together. Blaqnmild did come to the commercial shoot, but since that he hasn't supported me.

Through it all every year I made sure to send him holiday wishes and especially his birthday wishes because I still consider him a friend and I know the truth. We talk here and there but not as often. When I asked him what's the problem, he would be like nothing B and I be like ok cool. Deep down inside I know there's something bothering him. I was his number one artist. I was one he shared things with. I was there through his relationship and the birth of his first child, the arguments and even took blame for him being away from home a lot.

Rumors are harmful and people would always spread them about me. I never expected to lose a friendship over a rumor. It's crazy because coming up we seen what both Cash Money and No Limit was going thru and said we would never play each other like that or play on people. If we make it, we would give them their worth. I always give people what's do to them. Even those that roll with me if I get extra, I take care of my people. When I win my team win. This is a reason I have a closed-door policy and ask my friends to watch who they share information with because everybody is not your friend and everybody is not for you. People won't help you build but would tear you down and try to build with the people you've been building with.

_Some of the same people I pitched ideas to thought I was crazy but when the ideas hit, they would come back. I'll be like I'm good and for some reason they don't respect that. Since the people I turn away be those who others know I had communication with would go and speak on me they would assume what's they say is true. It happens every time.

Anything don't go their way folks go out and try and damage my name. Instead of them finding a lane of their own, they waste time attacking me. Years and years of the same crap they should know themselves that it doesn't bother me. They know I'm numb to the foolishness when it comes to talking about me and bashing me. I don't even care anymore. What I care about is finding solutions to problems.

The reason I'm always on top is because I outthink those against me. While they are attacking me, I'm attacking a new project. I never turned on nobody in my company from a word someone told me about them. I'm to straight forward for that. You cannot and will not pick me. I will not allow anyone to pick me. When you weak you beat. History means more to me so I will not let you new people tell me anything about somebody I been running with. I may be 10th Ward Buck the entertainer but my name is Marlon Justin Horton Sr. and he's no fool. No homo but periodt lol!

When doing business make sure to record and write as much down as possible it's best to write it all down. Understand what the deal is about, what it covers and who's responsible for what. Make a contract from the notes then meet with the person or persons you're doing business with and go over it before signing. Always have someone to review the paperwork and have someone with you at the time of signing. Keep others out of your business. Whatever deal you have with a person or company is your business. Don't go out telling your business. Be sure to deliver on your word and make sure the other party produce as well. Don't allow someone on the outside to stir you away from a decision you feel is right for you. Maybe they are right but ask question like why you feel I shouldn't do this, or have you experienced that before.

Most people make decisions based on what they heard. A lot of failures are from listening to others. I've seen it hundreds of time where people would take advice from family and friends and lose. We love our family and friends, but they are not experts at everything. Do research, study find out as much as you can on your own because at the end of the day when and if it falls you will be stuck with the burden.

Your friends are your friends but keep that separate from business. They either support or don't there's no in between. Get rid of those that's not supporting. Don't be a fool, even if they think it's a bad idea it's yours and as a friend, they should support cause if it wins best believe they going to be there enjoying the success. I know because they were many times my so-called friends didn't agree with my plans but when I gave an event to celebrate it, they were there.

A problem I faced is that I didn't do these things and went off word of mouth and each time it caused a problem. I made mistakes that I don't want others to make.

People ask why I put my life on social media. Well it's because I've been through so much and seen so much that I want to share it so others can see another outlook on life and say if it looks that bad what Buck is doing then I'm not doing that or say I like how Buck did that, it's nice I need to do that.

Somebody must set examples and I feel I've accomplished enough to do so. Tune out what they said about me because there is no proof but look at my successes. It's more than enough to have credit to teach others the do's and dont's.

When it comes to information, I lead the pack in that. Anytime someone ask me for advice I shoot it over. Sometimes I'm there personally to give them a hand. The way social media runs people soak up the bad and drag it on and on but the moment you do something good it's like hey ok what's next. Just like the truth and lies. The truth is straight forward and lies get dragged on because it's a lie and it requires more info to support that lie. Once you tell one lie you must tell more to cover it up. Therefore, it goes on for a while. I get a lot of heat because when someone lie on me, I respond aggressively. I do so because people pick with me and I just let it go but after a while I just blow up.

The number of followers I have, it seems as if I start because most of my followers do follow those that pick with me but I'm not out here worrying about people beneath me. Before we judge and we shouldn't be judging but it's human nature. So, before we do so get to know a person. Figure things out on your own about them and don't allow others to make you feel a certain way about them. It's time to take ourselves back. Doing for us and not doing things to impress others. Those days are done. We must pull ourselves up before we can pull someone else up. We must speak for ourselves before we speak for others. We must back family before we back others. We must provide for our household before we put things in others household.

10th Ward Buck

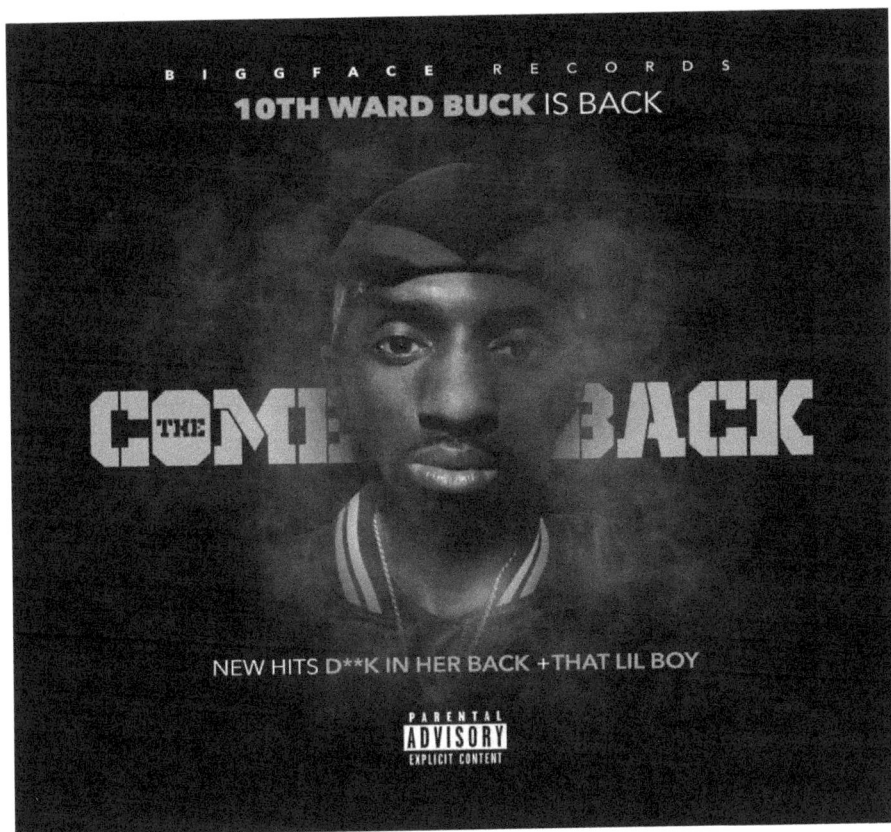

Chapter 4:

When it came to me entertaining, my community I was the go-to guy. I first started with making T-shirt's. One day a company came to my high school to fit all Juniors and Seniors for class rings. That day I missed so I had to go to the company's headquarters.

While there, I noticed that they also did our school T-shirt's. I then asked if I wanted to order my own shirts could I. They replied yes! So, I came up with a few designs and showed them to friends. I took the design that had the most likes and made a few sample shirts just for me.

I received so many inquiries about the shirts I made on my first order. Soon as I got the shirts they were sold. Order after order they would sell as fast as I got them. I then came up with a way to maximize my profits and have people buy more than 1 shirt. If I order two hundred white shirts, then I would only get one black just for me.

People love to be different so after seeing over 200 people with the same color shirt and then me with another it made me stand out. At that moment, people started to request different colors. My designs would change and as it got colder, I went from long sleeves to hoodies.

One day I got my order from the company and there was a slip from the company, wanted to contract with me which would make orders cheaper than what I was paying. I looked at the slip and called the company. Once I talked to the rep I went to the company and wow! I was spending way more than I would with them because this company was huge and had machines to do the work quickly. Not only did I save and made more money, but I was getting my product quicker. It went from an idea to a business. It was my first real business. I also used to sell candy in elementary school.

My business got bigger as group of people would ask me to do shirts for their clicks. Clicks are a group of people that represent that same thing. Most call them gangs but we were that. This business was made more popular in the project.

On holidays I ordered new shirts and boom like that they're gone. I had a business and didn't even know it. I was doing it for fun. I then invested in my own equipment. I attended a class where if you complete you get a grant and loan to start your own business. I completed it with flying colors. The things they would teach I'll answer quickly.

Once I received my checks, I brought all the things I needed and found a place to rent. I moved all my items in the place and the next day when I went back to move things in place all my things were gone! Everything was stolen! This was the start of my credit going bad because I just got a loan for expensive equipment and did not have the money to pay it back.

I asked the landlord and the neighbors, and they all said they didn't know what happened but between the two of them, one of them if not both knew. I wasn't sure if I was ready for that anyway because I'm too out going and can't see my myself locked down all day. So as y'all see all these

T-shirt shops around town know I been doing it since the late 90's.

I talk to people all the time and tell them if you don't go forward with your vision you won't grow. And what I mean is you must believe in yourself. Whatever it is you want to do go for it. Stop looking for validation all the time. Don't be afraid to take risk. Believe in you. In order to get through you must go through. You will not know the ending results until you try it. Just because something happened a certain way to someone else doesn't mean it will go that same way for you. Important fact, whatever it is you want to do make sure it's something you live and passionate about. Cause if it's something you don't find interested you would get tired of it, unfocused and it will fail. But when you do something you love no matter the outcome you still feel good about it and stay trying to find a way to get others in. Do what you love, go for it.

The T-shirt business made me more popular in and around my community. I took the attention I had and started giving bus rides to the Airline skating rink. Before then, people would try to make things like that happen but more than often it failed. I was tired of hearing that something should be given for our community so after so many ideas I choose the skate rink. I went there to asked them about giving a function and making money off the door. They told me they had this thing called a fund raiser, where the group would bring in people to this facility and they would give them half of the profits. At the time the cost was $6 per person so $3 for the rink and $3 for that program. I asked if I charged $15 how would that work, they said we just take out $3 and you keep the rest. I was sold. That first night I made $14,000! Again, and again I would do it.

Then I started doing holidays with concerts. It was everything. When I tell you, I had every bounce artist that was hot at the time performing. Averaging 15,00 people an event. That made me bigger because not only was my hood showing up but others as well. It would be the talk at schools.

So, from my hood to the schools the word was out about my skating parties. I was living it up at 17! I had a problem, and it was cars. There was this place called Volunteer of America where they sold old cars. I would always get one, but the problem was the amount of money I had to put in them. Sort of like y'all do with y'all taxes, spend the whole check on a lemon. The skate rink was a huge success.

It started to go down because another guy came and salted my name with the police. At that time the owner was like whatever the police said he was with it. They then started to take away my profits making it 50/50, so if I charged $15, they get $7.50 to them dropping the price back to $6 then the guy who salted me asked for a smaller amount off the door.

I introduced him to the owners before, so his story seemed true to them at the time just because they assumed him being affiliated with me, he knew what he was talking about. Truth is he wanted me out the way so he can do what I was doing and that's just what he did!

Somehow, it failed and now the rink themselves have a Bounce night. This is when I first started to notice the pictures that were painted of me. I met with the manager and he told me some things of which they heard wasn't true.

Then I had a talk with the police who was over the detail, it was so much that was said it was hard for me to defend myself. What hurted the most is all the business I bought them and the friends we made it should have been brought to my attention earlier of what was said about me. I really hated when I got somebody else charge.

Apparently, a group of guys had guns and it was told to the police that it was my people. Boy I was heated! I really fucking hate to be accused of shit that don't have anything to do with me. It was hard but I had to take the blame. Taking the blame wasn't easy because I still had to attend that place. When I was there, I didn't even want to look the manager nor the police in the face. I was disgusted. This is the main reason I don't listen to people and their word, I need proof. Don't tell me what you heard tell me what you saw.

Here it is us as a people who been thru enough already fighting with each other. The crazy part it's something I created. People need to learn to stay in their own lane and create their own things. Stop jumping on somebody else's wave and trying to take over. There's plenty of money for us all. We don't need to fight, come together and make it together.

Even though my skating events came to an end there we many positives I took away. I've learned and met a lot of people.

One person that I met was Lucky Johnson. Lucky is the CEO of Biggface records. Lucky didn't have a bounce artist on his label, but he had a lot of dancers. His dancers would practice their routines off my music daily. The day Lucky came was a day where I had a concert and his group asked if he could bring them there.

Our first meeting was short, a hi and eye contact exchange. I called him a few days later and we hooked up to discuss plans on me signing with his label. As the time went on, others seen us run together and they would tell me not to hang or sign with Lucky. It was hard for me to listen to them because it was the same people that wanted me to run with them. It's amazing how people would talk bad about a person just for attention or company. Some of these same people would have conversation with Lucky. I kept my mouth closed but I wouldn't trust nothing they say or participate in any events they would do with Lucky.

Most of the time they would partner with Lucky so that he's responsible for paying me. When that happened if the event loses, I lose because being that Lucky is my friend, I wouldn't charge him. After so many times I just told him either get the money from them or I'm not participating and like a friend he came through. People pretend and make it seem like they want you to win but, in all reality, they are all for themselves. I noticed this with people that came around me and Lucky. If I had an idea for something or needed something form some of them, they wouldn't deliver but as soon as they needed me, they would contact Lucky and go that route. For about a year that would be the routine until I took notice. I was like bruh some of these same people coming to you are those that would block me of certain things are meant for me. We talked and laughed about it because we played it all out. I seen the bs they were pulling. Nothing none of them said about lucky was true on my behalf. We jumped in the music business and made a name for ourselves.

Lucky was there for me every step of the way. He was even there for my family and friends. From flat tires, to running out of gas to moving furniture Lucky showed up. Anybody else would have their hands out. Just like Lucky was there for me I delivered on helping him as well. Any and everything I did his name was in it. That branded him more with the younger generation because he was already known with the older. Lucky who goes by Lucky Johnson have been entertaining as well. He loves comedy.

One day my friend Tracy came to New Orleans and asked if I wanted a role in this movie she was casting for, I declined but said I have a friend who I want to introduce you to and it would be great. I declined at the time because I had relationship issues and I wanted nothing but to make that work. Tracy asked if he can come that same day and Lucky showed up. This would restart his acting career. From there he got an agent and now he's at the top of his acting game. I also helped Lucky get into college and not only did he attend he graduated, not only did he graduated he ran for and won Mr. Delgado. It's funny because I would ask him to do certain as a challenge and he would be up for it. At the time I thought it would be impossible for us to make some noise of him being Mr. Delgado because of all the different walks of life. Not Lucky, he was like "where do I sign up". I laughed to myself like look what I started. Well Lucky he signed up, ran and won.

My next idea was doing a stage play. We did it and it was the first bounce stage play. We called it "Catch that Beat". We did 3 nights and they all were sold out. Since 2003 together we've been making headlines in our city and still to this day as others have come and gone, we're still here entertaining the people. All this goes to say you can't listen to what people say about another person all the time you must see for yourself.

Teamwork makes the dream work is my motto. It takes a team just like it takes a village to raise a child. You have to build a team then attack your plans to achieve your goals. Too often I see people glorify themselves in which they have the right, but you don't do that and not acknowledge those that helped you along the way. You will set yourself up for failure and or your team will be moving on from you.

I know what a team can do and that's why I always incorporate others into my plans even if I can do it on my own. It's about building and with others onboard you build faster and stronger. Now you just don't put anyone on your team. Some people are just for themselves, so you have to do some kind of research before teaming up with certain people. This has been my problem. M popularity would attract people who want to live off me or who wanted attention. These same people would find it hard to do simple things. Take a picture of me, pass out flyers and collect money at the door. They would have big heads as if those things were beneath them. Time after time they would do this or fuss with each other about who should do it. It got to a point where I'll only give them things or money when they work for them. I then begin to phase them out. There was no need to have people around me living for free when I'm not only doing all the work but paying all the bills. We have to eventuate the people around us from family to friends and our relationship. It makes no sense to keep people around who's not going to help you go forward. Don't be afraid to let go. Letting go gives you a piece of mind.

I noticed I was always angry and upset around certain people, but it would be mood swings. The reason for the mood swings was I'll just up and think about that certain person that wanted to be around but didn't want to help on the last event. As I stated and always say, they won't be there doing the building, but they'll show up for the grand opening. How many family members and friends we told about our ideas and how many supported? We have to take noticed of what's real and what's fake. There are more people on the outside who've helped me versus those who were in my company.

Lucky Johnson of Biggface Records, Slam of Sweetsticky stuff bundles, Trey of Trey Trending massage, Masd of Mobile City 504 phone repair, Mike of Fun in the Sun NOLA, Celina Of Crescent City taxes, Paige of Paige

Taxes, Sess 45 of Nuthin but fire Records, T Carter of Carternation are people who at one point of my life helped me at a time where I really needed help.

Celina Of Crescent city met me and Lucky as she relocated to New Orleans and became a friend of ours. When she first came down, we informed her on different things. Later, would become one we needed for business plans and help. I love her vibe and willingness to help and be involved in projects.

One other person that stands out when it comes to knowing what to do when having a business is Slam. Not only did he invest in my ideas he invested in a business I started for my ex. He gave me so much info. The best thing he said is you can't always employ family and friends. Boy was this true. Looking back on all the businesses I had there were family and friends' employees. He would then go on by saying sometimes you have to be at the workplace yourself and if you don't have the time to manage your own business don't start it cause that's an easy way for theft to happen.

I went over to his store and watch how he operated and man it was so smooth. He had things down packed. There were no arguments, disagreements. Bruh, I wish I had this knowledge at the beginning. He also stated sometimes you must pay for information so you might open a business and close just make sure to take away things you can learn from. Going to him for an investment turned out to be much more. You can either learn from your mistakes or lose all around. Still to this day I follow and mock the things he does. The way he advertises, how he run his business and how he allows you to talk first then correct or help you find a better solution for your problem. You never know who can influence you educationally unless you open. That's one thing I never did, because people were only about them but when Slam was like you can share anything with me because it makes no sense of me helping if I don't know what's happening so I opened up and told him as much as I could even some of my personal life experiences because I didn't want him in the blind of things social media world make me out to be. Although some things didn't go as planned, we both took away things that we will use going forward. It's all about team work. Build a team, build the right team and attack the plan not each other. Teamwork makes the dream work!

New is better at times that's why I don't go by the no new friends' motto. Sometimes you must move on, relocate or change your circle in order to obtain success. I like meeting new people. You can learn from others and sometimes it be people who have experienced the same thing you did. When starting a business or entertaining people you have to be outgoing. You have to open up. These are the people that will be your supporters. If you don't have a support system you have nothing.

Old friends are often intimidated when you meet new people. If they were a real friend, they would understand their place and your mission. Don't get caught up in that I don't need new friends' crap. New friends can be the ones you really need to help you along your journey while old friends are doing the same ole things. If you do what you've always been doing, then you going to get what you've always been getting. Try it, open up. Look for more, want more. I'm not saying go out and consider everyone you meet a friend but go out and find those that world become a good friend and one that you both can't benefit from. I'm always looking for business ventures from other people, but I don't accept them all. I take my time and I see what they mission is and if in fact they have a positive mission and not one that's to ride my boat. I'm at that point in my life where if I did enough lose to keep losing. I'm not at that point where I benefit off of my loses and other things I've been through.

Don't fall for the same things. If it didn't work, it's ok to give it another shot but after so many shots you have to analyze the situation and attack it a different way and sometimes it may be adding or subtracting something. We continue to lose because we try the same thing over and over with the same strategy. Write down your plans and goals. On that list look at what's working and what's not. Study another business that's doing the same thing you're doing. You have to see what's working for them.

Sometimes you have to use their same strategy until you can tweak it to your own way. When people ask me about starting a business, I always say go with something you are passionate about, something you are good at doing and some you have knowledge about. This is the best information anyone can be given.

When you jump into something without knowledge you lose. Don't ever do that! Now, it's ok to want to start a business you know nothing about, but you must research it first. This is where help from friends come in. Although you could but try not to attack things alone. Call up a friend or family member. Let the know what you are doing and get them involved with your learning process.

You can even see if a business owner that does what you want to do will give you information. Even though you will be doing the same thing, there's always someone out there who's willing to help. Pride have to be put to the side. The fear of rejection has to be put to the side and the thought of failure has to be as well. We all know what can happen, but we must believe in what we want to happen. The best thing you can do for yourself is believe in you. If you don't, then who will?

A Badly Painted Picture

VOTE

MARLON "BUCK"

HORTON

COUNCIL DISTRICT B #2

Chapter 5:

10th Ward Buck

I can't mention friends without mentioning my late friend, Dennis Floyd aka Flo. Flo lit up every place he would enter. He was the life of the party. No matter where or how many people was there, Flo knew how to change the tempo and get the people up and partying.

When it came to entertaining, he was in a class of his own. Flo loved to dance, and he was good at it. No matter the situation Flo made a dance for it. It started way back in elementary when we were attending Kingsley House. Whenever he would get a victory, he would have a celebration dance. Celebrations in football games are popular now but we been doing that.

The best time was when we were swimming and while in the race, Flo would bust out a lil 1, 2 wobble lol. When I tell you, he can roll! Music was his thing. He would always make up lil melodies and make a song around them.

What he was most known for was his song "you ain't never had a trade with a fire bald head, River Garden Floyd 10th Ward Driveway" it was fire. Everywhere we went people would holla the chant to him.

When I introduced him to social media we quickly took over. At first, he feared being on the social media sites with all the exposure I had. Flo was afraid of what the people was going to say. He concluded and said fuck it and boom when he jumped, in it took off.

At the time, I was doing a stage play and needed a female character to play alongside me as Be'Sha.

I then told him he should do it and just like that Flo'Esha was born!

We started a slogan known as "fuck them and they never did like me", put it on T-shirt's and sold hundreds. Everything we was touching was a success.

Flo loved the ladies and had one for every lil thing. One to buy food, another to cook the food, and one to wash his clothes! I mean he had it made and was living it up. Flo would tell them you have to make an appointment to see me lol.

Boy he was funny. He enjoyed them so much he would invite them all to his shows but wouldn't go in the crowd when they were there.

We were the first to start an Instagram show. At the time you could only upload videos 15 seconds at a time. It took a while just to upload 6 minutes of me and him acting up. We had to go to Starbucks or any place that had internet at a high speed.

Me as Be'Sha and Flo doing Flo'Esha, we would mimic everyday life and make fun of how females act in certain situations. It was funny as shit. We took make up and put it in the wrong places or we applied to much. We also put it in our nose. The ladies loved Flo. We started doing stage plays and when I tell you we sold them out as fast as we got the tickets. Flo was like a kid with candy on show dates, he lived for every live show. He was so good he would do extra things in the show that we didn't even practice catching me off guard and having me laughing. Y'all know I'm always ahead of the game and thinking.

I told Flo you have to record music. At one time, he was scared of the reaction he would get from the people. He wouldn't have a problem doing it on social media but live in front people he wasn't ready for that.

So, one of the songs I wrote for him I recorded myself and did the video and the reaction from that was sweet. He saw the attention I was getting off the song I wrote for him and was like that could have been me. He then asked when I was going back to the studio.

He would end up recording 4th Ward Patty, Where is D Boys and 8th Ward Animal. They all were hits! From there I couldn't get him to stop rapping.

Flo was good at being unbothered. He would constantly say fuck them to every situation. There were things we would discuss but he'll be like it would be ok let's just do this or that and it would die out. He wasn't here for bs! We had it all. We had the attention of the city and we were doing shows. The show was in high demand, which meant we had to move in an apartment together so we could keep up with the demand.

In the beginning he had a lot of issues in his personal life. But towards the end of his life I started to see happiness.

On the night of his murder we were in the car on the way home and he asked if I do not post we was at home but post we was at a club. Me not knowing why, I did as he said.

He was my friend, and me not question him, I did as he requested. Now I'm like I wished I would have asked him why, maybe it would have some info leading to the arrest of his murderer.

So, we grab a plate of food from one of his female friends and headed home. We walked in and placed our food in the microwave and sat on the couch to watch the basketball game. He got a call from a female to come outside.

About 10 minutes later I hear him screaming my name, followed by a big bam from the door as he ran into it before opening it! He ran straight to the kitchen followed by a guy with a huge gun pointed at him! I ran to the back and as soon as I got in the closet, I heard the gun shots.

Flo was heading for the back door, but he couldn't get out because the table we normally use for our show was blocking the exit.

Soon later, the police arrived. As they escorted me out the door there was my friend, laying shot to death by the table!

Nobody knows the motive not even me, but since I didn't talk to anyone about what happened they just started pointing fingers. Leading to the rejection of the family not wanting me at the funeral or being apart. The one person that was there and who understood as I told him everything, I knew was Flo brother Herb. Everybody else would believe he say she say.

This is my friend, we lived together and ran a business together. I wouldn't dare hurt a soul, let alone my friend! It was also rumoring that I started a go fund me account for him which also was a lie. The craziest lie was that I was selling T-shirt's, it's crazy because in our city when a person dies, we buy shirts in remembrance of them. So, if I did what was the problem? The T-shirt companies make money weekly off deaths.

Looking back, I see that any and everything was bought up to make me a suspect. What I did do on my own and no help was paid for a second line and DJ for 3 straight years on my own. There I gave shirts and fans away free. Lies and negative things always shield the truth and positivity.

Years later I'm able to finally share my side without all the confusion. This is what Flo would have wanted anyway. He would say "tell your side Buck baby" then say "fuck them" so in his honor fuck them! Here's my story about my friend Flo. A life taking too soon. We must embrace each other and celebrate each other while we are here living on earth. No one knows when their day is coming. Love one another and stick together.

I love New Orleans. It has its ups and downs but for the most the culture, I can't live without. The music, the food,

2nd lines, Mardi Gras and the Saints. It's hard to leave and not come back. Every time you turn around there's another event.

Our murder rate needs to decrease. At one time our city leaders blamed it on the housing projects, but years later and no more housing as they were back then there is still murders. It's amazing that with so much going on in our city on the positive side that our young men still engage in gun related crimes. We all have lost a loved one to guns so at some point we have to realize that we have to save ourselves from ourselves. We are fussing and fighting over females, who bumped who or who stepped on who shoe, who looked at who a certain way, who selling what on what block. All stupid shit.

I figured it out that it's all the mindset of those involved. I ran into problems with a few knuckle heads and what I have realized is that they have a lack of understanding. Something would happen and automatically they would point fingers at who they assumed to be responsible for that.

I'll say something like "homie I don't even know your baby momma" and his reply would be "boy fuck you, they said she was on your live, so you do know her". Bruh that's some crazy shit. It's been like that for years where my name would become the escape goat. Talking to these people I see it's their way or no way even though their way may be the wrong way. They have a point to prove and by any means necessary they are going to make something happen.

Their mindset is not set up to talk and resolve verbally it's set up to shoot. Once they are like that, it's hard to talk to them, and even if you do talk to them that's not what they want to hear. Therefore, we must do as much as we can to save our young boys before the streets get a hold of them.

This is also why I distance myself from old friends and new people who try to hang with me. I don't want their past to have me hurt. Sometimes people be in beef and wouldn't tell you and now you are in it by association. Mistaken identity and innocent people lives are being taken daily. Black on black crime is out of control! We need to pull this shit together and start enjoying life to the fullest.

We need to expose our kids to bigger and better things. Let them see other shit than inside the house and you going to 2nd lines and DJ's. Parents are at the front lines of it all.

How come tourist can come down and enjoy our city and we can't? It's a cycle that won't break unless you as parents start the process. My kids see me here and there and ask me about it and I inform them. I also take them places just so they can see other things that are outside of New Orleans. Some just want to run the streets and leave their kids inside instead of talking to their kids and getting them involved in activities. They treat their kids like dogs outside locked up to chains all day. How come you can spend time with a friend but never give your kids time and you wonder why you don't know what they're doing. It's time to reverse that shit.

I hate going to people house and not knowing they had kids because the kids are always inside or by a relative house. That is child neglect to me. I hate it! These children must spend their childhood locked up.

School functions gets no participation but every party and club event y'all be there. Some treat the person they in a relationship with better than their own children. These kids pick up fast these days and notice everything. Kids just don't suddenly disrespect their parents, it's the lack of love you have shown to them. You can expect respect from no one when you don't give it.

Children should stay in their place, but if they are being neglected and disrespected, eventually it would show.

Therefore, kids are quick to go by their grandparents or aunt home because inside their own home they're trapped. They are being neglect or given away as the first child but still have 2, 3 and a fourth child. They babysit their children not parent them. What I mean is they would lay up inside all day, talk in the phone and watch tv while the kids are inside bored but wants to scream at the kids when they run around. Like what do y'all expect? Get hold on your life and take care of your kids before you lose them to the streets. Watch your lil boys so they don't get caught in the jail system.

Also, watch your Lil girls so they don't be so fast in sexual activities. We have a beautiful city and can help make it better by bettering ourselves and raising our kids the right way.

10ᵗʰ Ward Buck

Raising a child can be hard and stressful at times but you must stay consistent and things will get easier as you go along. No matter how hard it may seem to you, keep pushing and keep going forward for your children.

I'm speaking from experience during my break up with my first baby mother, I had to raise four kids on my own it was hard, very hard being that I am an artist and entertainer at the same time.

There were days where I had an event and I had to find someone to watch my kids. Even though sometimes it would be last minute, I'd find a family member who will watch my kids. Watching children can be challenging so sometimes I have to pay others to watch my kids. People take for granite how hard raising a child can be. I struggled during the first 6 to 7 months to raise my 4 kids. When I tell you, it was rough it was rough! I had to raise one boy and three little girls.

My oldest son Marlon Junior a.k.a. MJ was not the problem. It was trying to raise three little girls. I was lost I didn't know what to do at times when their hair was out of place, I was like what the hell am I supposed to do! All I knew was getting their hair braided. However, I was tired of it and so was My Girlfriend. They wanted it to be just like other little girls who wore their natural hair. I noticed getting braids in their head constantly was pulling their hair out. During that time, I recently opened a restaurant called Finger Licking Wings. I was trying to figure it all out. As long as they were in school, I was OK but during those days it seems as if the school hours was going by fast. I had to run manage and work my restaurant while planning each day when my children get out of school. At that time, their mother wanted to run the streets.

With me doing so much in the entertainment business in New Orleans, I was always busy, so I understand the reason their mother wanted to get out and experience life without being under me all the time. However, I did not like how she just up and left us. It is one thing to leave me, but it's another to leave your children. What made it harder was when my kids would ask for their mother. I had no answer, matter of a fact, that that question made me tear each time.

As the days went by, I think about that question and how it still does hurt me. I remember this day when my daughter Marshawn asked; She said, "daddy why my mama can't go on the field trips with me like my friend mama do?"

When I tell you that shit cuts like a knife! Trying to be there for your kids and not having answers for their questions hurts. At this point, I wanted nothing but for my kids to have some communication with their mother. I wasn't worried about me and their mother being in a relationship anymore or even having a conversation, I just wanted her to be in our children's lives. Although at that time the kids were better off with me, she still could have made a way and time for them.

Not only was I struggling to be a full-time parent I was struggling financially, I had just invested in a brand new car a restaurant and recently paid the bills in the house we were staying in. Her decision to leave at that time was bad. I've never imagined this happening to me, and I wouldn't wish this on anyone. You can be there for a person and that same person can be wanting to turn around and walk out your life. It wasn't me, it was the influences of people on her of which she was seeing.

Now, I don't blame what my kids' mother was doing on others, however, what they exposed her to had an effect on her. She will see them, go out and party, have a good time. They would not have their kids so she would do the same thing. Day in and day out I will see pictures of their mother at event and those same days she wouldn't reach out and call us.

After almost a year of this I decided to call up a talk show called "The Test." The test at that time was looking for people who was going through the same situation I was going through. I felt as if it was meant for me to call the show. Everything that was advertised on the show was everything I was going through.

So, we went on the show to explain our situation, and it didn't change anything. You cannot force anyone to be a parent do you have to be willing to step up all in their own.

A long-lasting relationship depends on relating. It starts off with you liking another person but then it goes into love and most importantly having things in common. What I noticed about my relationships is that the women I would date would not be on the same level as I am when it comes to business. They would be into me and love me however, when it came to the things I do, it would not interest them. All day I will write and think about business ventures and all day they were out and about clubbing. Now the club thing is not a problem. The problem was damn wasting time worrying about a party instead of helping me succeed in whatever business I'm planning on doing. I mean I am the breadwinner, the provider etc. So be my backbone and help me to help us. They say behind every successful man is a strong woman. That's all I wanted was a woman who would be by my side and catch my bag when I would fall.

In so many words I was asking for a mature woman. Some people say maturity comes with age however I have seen some younger women act more mature than women older than they are. People always say Buck get you an older woman. I laugh all the time, I know people are here to help me and people want to see me succeed. So sometimes I think they have thoughts into consideration but a whole lot of other times I just laugh. You know basically be funny at times and sometimes you know the truth come through a joke! You know me I'm not about to hide up so when people tell me things I listen.

One rumor I would love to chill is the rumor that I always mess with younger women. Boy, when I hit it and laugh and laugh and I laughed some more not to throw anyone under the bus but some of these females are a mess and are still messing with men older than me. It's just my name my name, it not only ring bells but it causes havoc. People just don't let me live. I mean I can be doing the same thing my neighbor is doing but sis it's me it's no good. People put me on this high pedestal, they put me up high so high that when I am doing something natural... human nature is unexpected to them, so they be like Buck is tripping. I'll be like damn let me live I'm human too and I react to things good or bad as well. I have feelings just like you all. There's only one person that can judge us so when people make remarks about me, say things to try to make me mad or make me look bad, I brush that shit off. I brushes it off like I don't care what other people are saying about me, I don't! I never do, I never will because if you don't know me you have nothing to say about me at all.

It is the image that was portray about me is the bashing of me on mad day from others that just make people want to judge me. But you can't judge a person off what you heard, what I say all the time is don't tell me what you heard, tell me what you saw. When you approach me and the words that comes out of your mouth is blocked, that alone makes me want to get you out all the way. Because not everything we hear is true! Believe what you see don't believe what you heard until you can prove that yourself.

This has been another issue in my relationships where people would run to the female who I am talking to and tell them things about me not said that they saw those things but saying I heard those things. After so many rumors and so many people in their ear about me, of course that would start the disliking of me. So, you have the factor of us not being on the same page businesswise and you have us not being on the same page through what they hear from other people things I can't control. What I tried to get them to understand is that not everything that comes to you is true. Some people are jealous of what you have and jealous of us as a couple because of the way we present ourselves and things that we have accomplished. People have to realize that everybody is not your friend because a friend wouldn't be jealous of you and a friend will not envy your relationship. They won't take you away from what you have and what you have is; a home, a good man, he provides, he cooks clean, wash, and make sure you straight and that we have a roof over our head.

This is where I see for a relationship to work you have to relate, yet the happenings in common we have to have the willingness to understand. You have to agree to disagree however, you must keep outsiders out of your relationship and deal with the person you are in a relationship accordingly. You go behind closed doors you keep that door closed and whatever is happening, you keep it there.

I know for a fact that if my girlfriend would not share our business with her friends then her friends would not look at me the way they were looking at me, as if I am using her. I cheated on her I did not have the time to do that at all, not saying that I was perfect, not saying that I've never cheated not saying that I've never had a conversation with a girl outside. All I'm saying is whatever we go through should stay with us and we need to deal with that not your friends.

When you let friends take over your relationship it's over it's a failed relationship because you're not in control anymore. It's like anything your friends say will influence you and you would believe them over the person you were in a relationship with, that needs to stop. It's time we keep

BE ON THE SHOW

Do you need to put someone to **The Test**?

SUBMIT YOUR STORY

PARTY MOM OR PROSTITUTE?

Tuesday:

Marion says his ex-girlfriend, Raushawn, neglects their four children because she is always out partying – and sleeping with men for money! Raushawn admits she likes to go out but she denies being a prostitute. You won't believe where she says she gets her cash! Don't miss her confession. And, a woman wants to prove to her husband that she is faithful, after he found a pair of men's boxers – that weren't his! Don't miss what The Test reveals.

Monday-Friday
Check Your Local Listings

MUST-SEE VIDEOS

View All Videos

"Is Your Baby My Nephew Or My Brother?..."
She says her brother's ex-girlfriend destroyed her family!

Party Mom or Prostitute?
He says his ex-girlfriend neglects their four children because she is always out partying.

"I Had a Baby with Someone Else, but N..."
She says she caught him cheating before and wants to know if he's at it again.

The Test Moments
Get the truth – and then some on The Test!

Web Exclusive: "Tan Mom"
Never-before-seen footage of "Tan Mom," Patricia, and her husband.

Meet the Host: Kirk Fox
TV personality and host of The Test, Kirk Fox, shares his thoughts on the exciting new daytime talk show.

BE ON THE SHOW

Do You Need a DNA Test?

Want to Drug Test a Loved One?

Is Your Mate Having an Affair?

L.A. Only: Put Someone to The Test!

Hosted by TV personality Kirk Fox, The Test is a one-hour conflict resolution talk show that will use lie detector and DNA tests to settle relationship and paternity disputes among the guests.

BE IN THE AUDIENCE →

our business to ourselves and as I stated before deal with our relationship behind closed doors between us and no one else.

Chapter 6

10th Ward Buck

Hurricane Katrina for me turned out to be a good day. In 2003, I recorded a song called "Faster". It was the hardest song on both radio station at the time. Q93 and 104.5.

And in 2004 I recorded a song called "Drop and Give Me 50." I feel as if I was at the top of the Bounce game and that I went as far as I can go or at least I thought I would go.

In 2005 Hurricane Katrina hit New Orleans. I was living on the second floor in the Willowbrook Apartments with my first baby mother. Not knowing the damages Katrina would cause us. It flooded Uptown. It flooded in New Orleans East, at that time I had two vehicles and was not sure where to park my cars, in the East or Uptown.

Well everything got flooded; my Camaro, my party van, and my food truck. We were stuck for three days we had to make a bootleg Barbecue grill. We took the bottom part from under the oven of the stove and took the racks out of the oven and placed it on top and that's how we cooked our food.

When they did come to rescue us, we had to cut a hole in the roof on the third floor of the apartments to get on the roof so that we can be rescued. On the roof was me, my girlfriend, my friend Jeremy, and an elderly couple. The helicopter came and it only picked up the elderly couple and my girlfriend, leaving me and my friend to spend about six more hours trapped in the apartment. When we finally got rescued, we were brought on Veterans where everyone else who have been rescue were placed.

Scared, dirty, and nervous I walked around looking for my girlfriend. It was a sight to see... not know where she was in the crowd of people. I had become desperate to find her. I didn't hear her voice call my name and looked back and there she was. That was the best feeling in the world! It was good we found each other before boarding a bus because they were just throwing us on a bus, any bus just to get out of town!

We then boarded a bus that first took us to Baton Rouge but once we got there, there were police officers with guns! They had big guns and said that we could not get off the bus there. So, the bus took off a few hours later we were in Houston. The bus drove up and unload at the Astrodome.

There were people everywhere! People were crying everywhere, it was very sad as people were trying to use phones to contact their loved ones. Others had tears of joy when they got in contact with their loved ones, and others crying when they heard the news that a loved one or friend has died in the hurricane.

We stayed there about two or three days before our family took us in. We were grateful to have someone to take us in because we were able to do normal things like eat, sleep well, take bath and wash clothes. However, the family was real strick. Being that we come from having our own place we were not used to people telling us what we can do and what we cannot do. But most importantly the time that we had to come inside. Now it is their house and their rules, however, they wanted us inside by 5 and 6 PM! That wasn't no good for us we would need more than enough time to be out searching for people who were missing and researching on what do we need to do to contact Fema and all those other agencies for us to be able to live right.

Living with those people, even though we can eat, take a bath and wash clothes, was like the people at the astrodome living with them was like being in jail. I mean we were being treated like children.

So, one day we both decided to run away! We went back to the Astrodome which was perfect because that's where all the help was. Fema and Red Cross was there to help with housing assistance. Just about everything we needed to get our life back in order was at the Astrodome. We signed up for a program that put us in that apartment, and we will live there for about a year.

Once we got situated in the apartment our life began to get back. The feel of being at home started to come back. The feeling was we had our own club night at a club called Maxi's and Coco Loco at both clubs. So, we were able to get out and enjoy ourselves with other people from the city.

During the last three months in Houston, I went back and forward from Houston to Baton Rouge with my friend Lucky Johnson. Baton Rouge was the next step to getting back to New Orleans. Lucky had a Four Plex apartments in Baton Rouge, so after going back there for what we finally packed up and moved to Baton Rouge. In the middle of moving from Houston we found out that my girlfriend was pregnant with me and her first. We relocated to Baton

Rouge for about three months then moving into a trailer in New Orleans. It was a must I get back home.

In most areas of the city it was a ghost town, but Uptown was up and running like nothing happened.

Time went to go on as we lived in the trailer then an opportunity came which allowed us to move out of the trailer and into a house in the eight Ward of New Orleans.

As we moved in 2007 and 2008, we were on our second child, a little girl. This house and eight walls will always be with me, this is where I got the good news that my song Drop and Give Me 50 was going all the way With Mike Jones and Hurricane Chris. I will never forget that day when I got the phone call from Mike Jones saying that he remixed my song and wanted me to hear his version.

So, we talked game he played this song and I was like yes yes that's it is a hit! The sound of it the way it came on they really did their thing on that track.

Hurricane Katrina not only blew us away from the city, it also blew our culture and our music away. It helped my music crossover it also helped others get a feel of our music. Houston, for instants our music has been played so much out there that most of the Houston people have taken a liking to it. Now I have an audience in Houston!

Since then, I've taken many trips to Houston to perform my music. There are a lot of people from New Orleans who still live in Houston so just like they crave for their food they crave for their music. I am thankful that I am one who can entertain them.

When Hurricane Katrina came my music was at the top of the bounce music game. So, when they left, they left on my music. My social media site also help me out. As I work and put things back in order, I will upload it to social media for others to see. And like a charm it worked!

Those that were away really tuned in to see my transition and to see how I made things work. When it comes to business and doing things the right way, people knew and believed in me that I will get it right and do it right because like before I've always done it right.

My story is interesting, so I do follow along just to see what I'm up to and what am I going to do next. They love you they hate you they hate you they love you but no matter what, they will still watch. That's one thing I've learned in this entertainment business is that no matter what, people will talk about you. Being talked about comes with that depression. It took me some time to understand why but once I caught a hold on to what was happening, I started to tune it out and now that he says she say is numb to me. I'm so used of the name calling, the bashing.

I'm like oh well let them keep talking they just constantly building me up! I think those things that they say to me and about me, I put them under my feet. I stepped on it and it raises me up. You can't be in this business and take things personal, there are people who don't know you.

There are people who just don't like you and won't like you, you must build off that.

Hurricane Katrina have taught me that and so many other things. I wish that I could have experienced these things without the destruction that Hurricane Katrina had caused us. We can't question God, all we can do is be grateful and be thankful for any and everything he has blessed us with!

There is no place like home but there is also no place like New Orleans! I know people may think they have the best city the best whatever but when it comes down to the best... know all of this is the best! When you talk about food, parties, festivals, Second lines …. you name it when it comes to throwing down a no city like New Orleans! PERIODDDDD!

New Orleans is the country no scratch that New Orleans is the world, it is a continent of its own LOL. When you think of Bourbon St, Bourbon St alone give you a taste of what we love. We can have a party any day of the week and it's going down, I mean it is going down.

This is why is why it is hard to move away from New Orleans. This is why it's hard to stay away from New Orleans. Hurricane Katrina forced me out but at the same time I made my way back.

Years later, I started to make new music, from 2017 until 2019 I was back or forward from New Orleans to

Houston doing events. My Instagram and my music kept me relevant. Also, the people that's in Houston couldn't get enough of it so when it was brought to them in Houston from then success happened.

So late 2018 I decided that I was going to move to Houston. My plan was to still do those parties and book more parties. So, everything was looking good I got the apartment and I also got the space for the store but as I moved forward, there were days when I was alone. I was away from my kids I wasn't used to being away from them that long and they weren't used to me being away. It was like everything just started to crash down mid to late when I had to think about my kids. Every time my kids needed something I was there every time something needed to happen for them, I was there.

I try and move and get settled but it's like it got worse my kids knew daddy was not around. So, you know what they started to act out in school started to get in trouble especially my oldest son, he knows how to get me there. He knew how to get me around he will purposely do things so when I am in town I'm forced to come and get them from school. His behavior was good it was OK shall I say however, when I left him with his mama, he got worse.

I mean every other day every day he was getting in trouble getting put out the class not doing his work not doing his homework, just not doing everything that he should've been doing. My son is old enough to know better.

The move to Houston was always on my mind, however, I didn't think it out and did not write it down. I did have a plan and an opportunity presented itself for me to move. I just left, got my stuff, packed it up, threw some stuff away, gave some stuff away and I was gone!

I felt bad, I abandon my children even though my move was for a good cause, it's a benefit to all of us in the long run. I feel it was abandonment because I left them and that I wasn't there.

Every time I came back to the city from Houston, I will see my kids and it wouldn't be up to par. I hated it and it made me mad. Uniforms would be dirty, too small shoes, and socks would be mitching match. My daughter's hair will be picky if not for me my son wouldn't even get a haircut.

People think that buying children clothes that it's considered parenting. Come on now that's not even half of it. Buying kids clothes is a responsibility, so don't think just because you buy your kids clothes that you are taking care of them. Well that's how my children's mother think.

My kids are out going children and what I mean by that is that they like to explore, they like to go out, they like to do things. Their mother does not grant them that. For years the burden of taking care of our children have fallen on me. What I mean by burden is that I can't move on and do things, I have to take care of the household because I'm not getting the support from my children's mother.

10th Ward Buck

Taking care of children like I see is our responsibility, but it's a burden and sometimes it doesn't even have to be a burden.

I am a musician, I am an actor, and entertainer so at times it's hard for me to get to my events and find a babysitter. Most of my events are last minute and easy payouts.

You would think that the parent with the least amount of time with the children would at least pick up your slack when you need them to but no, not for me!

It wasn't working like that my first four kids' mother, after we split would live from this house to that house to her house to my sister's house back or forward to jail.

The system isn't set up to fully support men. Oh boy there would be times I'd go to different places to get my kids enrolled in something or get a document and it was rough. It's crazy because my name is on all the paper work. Which includes; the Birth Certificate. Oh, still I would be put through hoops to get the info I needed.

It's, 2019 things should be made simpler for us as men as far as get what we need for our children whatever records that we need. Trying to get this information gave me setbacks after sat back.   It was hard! I would go to the office present my ID I would present proof that the kids are with me. Still I would even present proof that the mother is in jail they would still ask me for certain things. One thing that really got to me that they asked me for was a letter from their mother, who was locked up at that time written from her signed stating that she authorizes me to have custody of our children.

Boy oh boy! You mean to tell me I would give y'all birth certificates with my name on it, I show you a document that the mother is locked up and you still deny me the records I need to enroll my kids at either school or after care! None of that made sense and the reply I would get each time is that they're only doing their job.

That made it seem to me that your job is to make my task harder when I have proof that these are my children and I have proof that they're staying with me.

Not all trouble came from the system. It comes from social media and sometimes businesses. One time, I was in a restaurant and this girl was supposed to be my server. It's crazy because when I walked in, I turned away, but I looked back quick enough to read… As she told the other worker oh, I'm not serving him.

Sad thing is you mean to tell me you built that much hatred up for me that you can't do your job in which you get paid for! She would rather risk that in order not to serve me or seat me, crazy.

I recalled, one time I went to a drive through, ordered my food and at the window one girl who I blocked off my Instagram. She got out raged! At first, I thought she was playing but then she moved the lineup and proceeded to

10ᵗʰ Ward Buck

come tell me all kind of crazy stuff. Like; "what are you doing here you think we want to serve you!

You're lucky your order is taken, because if I would've known it was you, we would've never taken your order."

When I tell you I was all kind of confused? People are sick in the head to allow social media to get to them and make them build up hate for another person.

I don't understand it, I really don't! I can't see myself just being upset in real life with someone that posted something on social media. I don't look at social media like real life! Now, some of it is real, don't get me wrong, however, it all has a twist.

I don't care who you are, so with that being said if something happened on social media, well that's where I leave it. But others take it to the head, to the grave, and really be upset. As I stated before nothing I post is intended to hurt or harm anyone. So, people must get out of their feelings, the best thing you should do if someone is posting things that you don't like is to unfollow them or block them. The fact that they don't follow, and they engage in what I do makes me furred to believe that at times they are looking for attention. If I post something about my life, then that's my life. If you had a problem with it instead, of you going off on me under my post you should call, text, or DM me.

I'm not one to judge. I tell you the truth I don't like it. People always want to judge you off what they heard. Seeing and hearing are two different things. Believe what you want, just don't judge no one off hearing things. I'm a firm believer of not judging at all. But if you are going to judge... judge on your own and not from other people's words.

Sometimes judging can get you caught up. What I mean by that you can't judge someone, and they'll be the total opposite of what you thought. I see a lot of people judging and not thinking.

People are so used old situations. To come up with their own theory of another person. Social media made it worse. I mean once you post something on Instagram, Twitter, Facebook, you name it people are quick to judge. Half of the time things that are posted isn't true. Delusional is what I call it. People often post things on their social media site to make it look like they have more than what they really do.

So, knowing that automatically you shouldn't want to judge because then you for sure are judging the wrong things. People judging me is what I used for my success. Everybody's always asking Buck how do you do it? Well I do it because I really don't do it, meaning entertaining people disliking me the fact that I don't entertain it wins.

As a matter of fact, I welcome it now, they say if you don't have haters then you don't have nothing. I have a lot of haters, so I have a lot of everything LOL. Bruh, when I tell you people will have dislike of you for the smallest things. People are so evil and Lord you see it daily on social media. It's crazy because people allow their jealousy feelings to show when other people display their success. I don't know

10ᵗʰ Ward Buck

how they do it, I mean hating takes too much energy. Hating takes too much time hating takes a lot of effort. So, for me to hate means I have to lose my energy and my time. I don't want to lose those two things and even if it didn't take just those two things, the way I couldn't just flat out be around here hating people just because they have this or just because they got that. Sometimes they hating the people right in your face! Crazy Ha? I never understood that but my theory about it is that people think because they are around you when you get success, they should have it too. It doesn't work like that. You have to work for success.

Also, you have to play your part. Maybe you did your part by helping your friend or relative reach their goal remember one thing you have to play your part. Remember, your role is yours, you cannot pass go.

If you are the manager then you are the teacher. Whatever it is you are not the student, so you have to let your student Blossom in peace. All this goes back to judging off what you heard because it takes those around you to influence others who really don't know you.

A Badly Painted Picture

Chapter 7

I'm into my kids because coming up I didn't have things other kids had. I know them having things would keep them happy. My kids have their own identities but when it comes to entertainment, I see me in all 6 of them. That's amazing cause you'll think that at least 1 would be different but they all are stage ready.

MJ, which is my oldest shy away at times because he doesn't click with his sisters like that, he's out numbered. When it was just him and my first daughter Maliah, it was all good.

MJ and Maliah would get on the camera all the time. When I first started my Instagram, it was with them two. As time went on, I had 2 other kids which are girls.

Now 3 girls and Maliah would spend more time with them. MJ then became good in sports so he's not with the girly stuff. Even if it's me on social media with my girls he feels as if it's girls because he's out numbered.

Most of the time when I'm live, people be like where's MJ? Well he be right there just off camera ducked off not to be seen. If it's just me, he would get on. My girls on the other hand loves it. They live for the entertainment. I'll be live and in the mix of me doing something and they would just join in and take over the live. At times they would remind me to go live. This woke me up to knowing for sure that I must watch what I'm posting on the internet because my kids are watching. I'm glad that they are involved because there's no greater feeling than working with your kids.

People have their own reasons not to be involved with their kids, but when it comes to activities and field trips, I can't see me not being involved. Being a parent is a part of your child's childhood.

As adults, we raise our children and when we get older, they'll take care of us. When my kids give their thank you speeches after graduation and promotions I want to be mentioned as their help in getting them on the track to success.

If more parents would get involved with their kids, then we'll have more success stories. The kids love for their parents to be there. The one memory that plays in my mind often, is when my daughter Marshawn had a field trip and she couldn't get her momma to go. She came to me and ask, "daddy why my momma don't go on a field trips with me like my friend momma?" Boy that took my soul! I teared up because I understood her but couldn't give her an answer.

That's the part that gets me all the time. The fact that I can't answer every question that my kids ask, or do I tell them the truth about certain things?! I don't want to lead my kids wrong, so I tell them the truth and dance around other questions, if I feel they are not ready for the truth. It's always right to be truthful with your kids cause the have wondering minds and they'll ask until they get the right answer. One thing I don't want is them to build a perception of me as a liar. That's one thing no parent need because you should want your child to trust you.

10ᵗʰ Ward Buck

We want to assure our friends and relationship partners of trust, we should do the same thing for our kids. My kids are at an age where they try to be slick, they know the answer already, but they still ask to see what I'll say. Knowing that I will be truthful as possible. As I stated before, dance around whatever question I can and think they are not ready for that answer. It starts at home so no matter what make sure home feels like home for your kids so that they won't end up at somebody's else home looking for love or acceptance. When you give and show your kids love you wouldn't have a problem of them opening up because they trust you. No matter the situation I want my kids to feel ok to come to me rather than someone else and if it's something daddy can't do, we'll go see somebody else together.

Who are my kids? My first 4 kids are for Ro. Marlon Jr aka MJ is 12, Maliah is 11, Marshawn is 9 and Marley is 7. Number 5 is Deuce he 5 his mother is Ellie and Child 6 is Mason he's 3 and his Mother is Trelly. Yep 6 kids and 3 what we call Baby mommas.

MJ is into sports and games. He plays football, basketball and baseball. So, when it comes to outside activities, he's busy all year round. His best sport is football. From age 4 he was a star. He gets it from his daddy. Yes, I played sports and I was fast. I wasn't sure if he was any good but as a father, I still wanted him into some kind of activity. So, at age 4 I took him to Clay park to sign up for Lyon Center 5 & 6-year-old team and he made it.

His first year he made a name for himself and he was good. I had to make sure he stood out and looked good. I went to buying all kinds of accessories from gloves, socks, tights, headbands you name it. I had him looking like a star. Each game the opposing team would point him out like he's the only one we have to worry about. Those who've been following me for a while have seen him in action.

Maliah likes to explore. She's very different. She likes to create things and since this slime thing is popping that's all she watches is slime videos. Experimenting is her thing. She's on the dance team but as she gets older, I don't think she would be into that. She loves to be outside. No matter what it is she wants to do it outdoors. I think if she can sleep outside, she would!

Now Marshawn is the confusing one. She's very smart by the head and mouth lol. I don't see how this is happening. A sweet lil girl but very vocal. Very bossy and would tell you what's on her mind in a second. She's on the dance team and loves to dance. Her grades are outstanding and she's at the top of her class each year. Crazy attitude but smart so I don't know what career to give her.

Marley, my baby girl is the complete dancer. Now I know she would be some kind of dancer. She dances all day to any kind of beat or music. No matter where she goes if she hears music she's dancing. If she goes too long without hearing music she hums in her head. From my phone, to my YouTube account Marley dancing videos are everywhere.

Deuce is getting it together, he the one around us the least, so I see how he's quiet, but then he turns up. He's a music person. He likes to rap and watch YouTube. He's my twin and the only one I really see me in. Y'all say they all look like me, but I don't see it. But hey, at least for sure we see it in Deuce.

Finally, Mason. Mason is two hands full. From spilling things all over to cutting his own hair and trying to cook on the stove Mason is a problem! Now he's at the age where he can speak and boy that made him worst! You can't tell him nothing. If he isn't with it, he will tell you. He needs boot camp. He can be sweet at times but not for a long time. Just like the baby in all other families, he thinks he's entitled to other people's belongings. Nothing phases him. You try and scare him with the Maw Maw character, and he says I'll beat her up. He calls me Buck not daddy! We say Mason you are going by your Maw Maw and he would say no I'm staying by Buck. If he's by his Maw Maw they'll tell him he's going by Margie and he'll reply no I want to go by Buck. Mason knows what he wants and it's his way or no way. Mason love him some Deuce! Once I make it to pick Mason up his first thing is where is Deuce. Although he's a lil devil he's very wise. I'm not sure where he wants to take his life but aaaaaa, we'll see later lol.

When it comes to parenting you should accept any child that's associated with your relationship even if it's not your child. As a parent, a father, a man, I accept any children that my girlfriend has had when meeting me. My ex Trelly have a Lil girl by the name of Daniyah who's 5. I took her in as my own. It's the right thing to do. In doing so I treated her like my own and didn't show favoritism between my kids and her. They all are treated the same way, I don't pick and choose. When I first met Daniyah she was a pain. She cried a lot, she was a cry baby. I couldn't stand it. She was spoiled behind her momma and wanted nothing to do with no one but her mother. Boy she had all kinds of thoughts running through my head like boy she lucky she not mine cause I'd whip that ass lol.

I mean being that we just met, there wasn't too much discipline I could do. When she would come over all she wants is to be under her momma and that was taking away from my time but as time went on, she adjusted, and I found out she just wanted her way. It took some time, but she grew out of it. You have other people who neglect their step kids. That's crazy because if you want me you have to accept my kids.

Most of us have seen a case where one doesn't accept the others child and for me that's sad. I mean what's the problem. No matter who the child is for when you accept their parent you should accept them. For those who still mess around with an individual who don't accept their child is sad too. You are smiling in a person face who dislike your child. You and your children are a package. People say a lot of shit about me but one thing they respect is how I take care of my children.

If you don't accept your boy/girlfriend's child, then you have no respect for them. That's just the flat-out truth.

10th Ward Buck

You can't be with me thinking you going to be disowning my kids, oh no it doesn't go like that around here. I rather be complete with my kids then to have a person around dividing us. Loving and caring for kids isn't hard it's just people are bitter and upset and use the kids to take their anger out on. As a step parent you should want unity in your home. Therefore, you should introduce yourself properly and show respect to the children and they'll give it right back. I learned that with Daniyah. I could have been mean towards her, but I wasn't and she learned me. She adjusted and allowed me to care for her.

I wouldn't want my kids to be neglected by their mothers' boyfriend, so I do my best to be the best man and father. I love being a father period. It gives me things to do and keeps me going not to mention I learn from my kids. I like to hear them tell stories and show me new lil things they've learned. Most questions are annoying, but I like them as well lol. What I don't like is when they jump on me asking and calling me at the same time. When I tell you, my kids have it bad. They call me all day. Daddy daddy daddy wait a few then daddy daddy daddy bruh I be so heated. In my head I be like call somebody else daddy sometimes lol. My parents ya'll understand me on this one. All in all, kids are kids and we as adults not just the parents all adults should accept them, love and care for them. As parents we all want the best for our kids.

This school year, I felt when it came to their schooling I didn't do enough. I was making an attempt to move to Houston and start over. The restart was to get things together so when my kids come to visit or stay it would be a nice place for them. I received an offer from a business in Houston that I couldn't refuse which was going to pay me two times a week. That would have been good, then I can be in New Orleans during the week.

This deal would have secured my rent, lights and living expenses. So, I moved forward on moving. Found a place to stay and got a commercial space to sell hair. As time went on, I lost constant contact with my kids. I was doing shows and working on my newly released cd "The Come Back".

There would be times where something happened with my kids and I couldn't be there to help. It was totally the opposite of what I thought would happen when it came to the care for my kids. Whenever they needed me before I was there and now that I was away in Houston I couldn't be there for their rescue. So, I started to get rooms in Harrah's in New Orleans. That way I'd have a place to stay so I can be around my kids.

It turned to me paying rent and utilities in Houston for nothing because I was in New Orleans more. I'll be in Houston on the weekend and in New Orleans Monday to Friday. It wasn't making sense, so I moved back home. My kids would call and call about every lil thing and it is aggravating more when there's nothing you can do. At times I would find myself shouting at them or hanging up in their face because I was upset that their mother wasn't tending to them.

10th Ward Buck

So, the frustration wasn't too much of my kids but towards their mother... lil baby what is you doing. I assumed with me getting away to make money for our kids' current situation and their future she'll be my support but the lack of her to care for them was hurting me. I can't make a move if I'm stuck with kids. What's crazy is I never have a problem watching them and when they with me I never call, I'll let them enjoy themselves here. Now on the other hand I'm constantly getting calls.

Now that I'm back things have fallen back into place. When we make decisions, we must take our children wellbeing in to account. Sometimes we move and those moves be too quick and not well thought out. Plans are to be made for every situation and that the children should be included.

My momma told me to stay involved with my kids because once you get comfortable with not being around them you lose touch. I took that a ran with it. It's just like a task once you stop doing it you get off track. You have to keep pushing even if your kids don't live with you make it your responsibility to see them or at least call them as much as possible. I've worked at many agencies dealing with kids and what I found out that most of them have behavioral problems because they lost contact with their parents. Kids want love and they want it from mom and dad first because that's who they know. That's who they expect it from. When something is happening, they want you as their parent to be there.

Another thing I learned is you can't make people be parents. Some people just don't care to do so. I can't stand to see people neglect their kids. Verbally and physically I can't stand it. They would tell the children all kinds of things and hit them when they're mad. That's the first thing a lot of parents do, take their frustration out on their kids. I've seen it too much and therefore I do my best to keep my kids around me. I would hate for them to be mistreated. I don't mistreat my kids so I'm not about to allow others to do it. If you make a child, then care for them but if that's not what you want to do then allow someone else to raise them.

Working with children helped me understand as an adult how to adjust to their feelings. What I mean by that is listening, allowing them to talk then finding a solution. Sometimes us as adults just tell the kids things without listening and most of the time the kids are right or have a valid point for a certain situation.

A lot of us parents would learn more if we just hear our kids out. Wrong is wrong but hear them out so you can teach them another way about going about things. Yelling don't prove anything! I sometimes get caught in doing that because I was used to doing it as an intimidating factor. I would fuss knowing I wouldn't do anything. I see others around them doing it as well.

We all raise our kids different, but I don't condone yelling and cussing at kids. I hate to see it especially in public. When I see it, I feel embarrassed for that child. Kids understand without yelling and cussing. Now, I know sometimes depending on the situation we yell and cuss but I'm talking about the parents that just be mad at everything and blame the kids which leads to mistreating them.

Here's a true factor, most parents miss treat their kids because of the other parent. I know one situation where this person can't stand one of her kids' father and that child gets the hardest time from her. I saw the mistreatment of this child and even over heard her say to the child I can't stand your ugly ass daddy. I was shocked, I'm like it's 2019 and this still exist where we mistreat our kids because of their fathers. Favoritism is what we call it. This is where a parent favor one child over another. I never understood that.

I can see education but to favor because of the child's father is ridiculous. Stop taking things out on your kids and just distance yourself from anything to do with the father. Most of the time when you still bitter and try to play catch back that person and what they've done stays on your mind. When it's time to move on you have to move on completely and that's even trying to play catch back. You have to walk away from everything.

The fact that you are still bitter and upset about your past relationship keeps you going as far as reminiscing on the past. Not letting go is affecting your relationship with your kids. Y'all put too much time into what's not anymore instead of focusing on the present and future. I'm one who have done that too often. I was so busy trying to make my relationship work I didn't want to have nothing to do with my kids. It was mental. I was stressed and wanted nothing but that person, so I didn't want to be bothered with nothing or no one. One thing I didn't do was take it out on my kids. That's not me, my problems are mine and that's the way I like to keep them.

At the children agency I worked at, the children would open up to me and share their life experiences. The way I carried myself and treated them allowed them to gain trust for me. As we talked, a lot of behavior situations came from their parents not communicating with them. They would talk about how they were treated but more on the fact that no one was listening to them. In order to understand you must listen. I have to preach this, let the kids talk. Listen to them and then find a solution. If you do jump on them immediately after they did something wrong. Just remember to go back in their room and have a parent to child talk with them.

10th Ward Buck

Chapter 8

10th Ward Buck

When it comes to my type of women, it's slim and trim.
Nothing against thick women because I love them all, I just
haven't graduated yet lol. We all have our preference of the

type of person we like. People come at me like it's a crime that I like slime females but it's just me. I don't dislike my thick women or my bbw's, I just need control.

When it comes to sex, I stay in my weight class because I feel like I'm the champ and for me to keep my belts I need to stay in a class where I'm the most dominant lmao. When it comes to boxing you must stay in your class, if you in a low class and move up to need to keep in mind you are fighting bigger people so that's how I view my sex life.

I have tried a thick woman before, but I wasn't ready for that and mainly because I wasn't used to it and the fact that she sorts of spiked me up. She would call and call and be like boy leave them lil thin ass girls alone and get you a thick woman. She would go on to say things like see that's your problem you need a woman with meat. I would laugh because people think I go through things because the females I deal with.

See I put in the public what I want them to know but not everything, so it's assumed I only mess with a certain people. I rather it like that anyway because some of the females I deal with don't like the attention nor do they want it.

So back to my thick girl one-night stand. She got in my head and we met up at the spot and made it happen. First, I like for the female to ride, however she was a bit heavy for me, then I like to hit from the back, but she said she wasn't ready for that she wanted to do her way the first time. Then

let me hit from the back the next time we do it, but in my mind, I was like she just doesn't know this is the first and last time. She told me she going to feel like a whore if she let me hit from the back the first time we do it lol.

But boy was I heated, because that's my favorite move and my finishing move. When she said that my other me told me; but Buck she is a whore lol. I'm crying laughing right now cause my other me knew we both was cheating so I'm like we both whores lmao.

Boy people do and say the most when they want their way. The crazy thing is at first, I couldn't even get hard cause I wasn't even supposed to be doing it with her. I was afraid of being busted because the meet up spot wasn't paparazzi free. However, we finished the business and she wasn't satisfying so she messed it up for my future thick women. Talking about, she going to feel like a whore if I hit from the back, girl if you don't take this dick.

Another opportunity came for me to redeem myself with a bbw and surprise I gave it a try and I bust down on thothiana. I gave her the business because she didn't mind feeling like a whore lol. When I tell you, I had her body moving like title waves! Boy was she really throwing it back. I think the first one wasn't nasty enough she just wanted me bad but I'm nasty and if I'm going to step out, I'm going all in. We are doing everything and I'm going in all holes opened. Don't judge me just turn this chapter lol.

The 2nd bbw was all that and a moon pie. After it was over, she even offered me some snacks. The first one was more in love with me and I don't like that cause when they in love with you skinny or thick they don't perform right. They try to stay on the low with their nastiness.

Now, I'm not blaming all my bbw's for her flaws I'm just saying it had an effect on me. Y'all people get in y'all feelings and just prejudice. I know somewhere one of my bbw's is saying boy come here I'll show you nasty lol. Hold on baby, I'm coming. So there, yes, I've had sex with thicker women I just didn't mention it.

When it comes to sex, I'm all in. I think my high sex drive comes from the lack of sex and the overload of work. I don't have many female friends and no sex partners "at the moment" lol got to quote that before it be some more Bs. I'm not the type to throw my name around and be into this girl and that one. One of the main reasons is I be just getting out of relationships and I don't be having a sexual attraction to only those I just got out a relationship with.

It's something how when you in a relationship you can be ready to have sex with this one and that one, but when you are going through a breakup that drive don't be the same. At least for me the drive doesn't be the same cause I don't use sex to get over another person nor do I use it to play catch back. I know some people don't give a shit they just want to have sex. Having sex with another person to play catch back don't make sense to me. I don't solve anything. All it proves is you can do what you want and fuck who you want but we all have that freedom. You are adding bodies on your list and creating future problems because that will always come up during mad day. Also, sex is temporary so while you are doing it now when that time is up you still have to face the facts of life in your relationship or friendship.

I love sex I really do. Back then me and my friends would have the male 3 somes with girls that we call a train, others say gang bang. Man, when I tell you that was the ish. Don't judge me, if I'm going tell it then I got to tell it all #usher lol.

So, coming up in the projects they would have girls liking me and my friends and couldn't choose so somehow, we end up having them at the same time. This way was better because I've heard another way where a dude would be having sex with a girl while the other is hiding and the first dude would say he's going to the bathroom and then the other would come out of hiding and have sex with the girl. Bruh I hated hearing that. It's wrong and sounds creepy. Me and my friends wasn't cutting no corners. We were the shit and if you wanted me and him then no need to choose to have us both.

Then as we got older it got better. There was this one girl who was in a relationship with both of us. She was beautiful and all. Now mind you we were for it because we didn't want to be in no relationship anyway because we were the shit so both of us messing with her kept people wondering. When they would ask, we would be like now how she mess with me if she messes with him? lol worked every time and the cool thing about her is she still let us do us. We were all just cool. No matter any situation, when we all have understanding is when the situation is perfectly fine. Some people may look down on it but we as people have the right to do what we please besides it was a friendly fun situation that I enjoyed. No matter what not everything in the world is approved on and you can't please everyone so please yourself so that's what I do. A train is a train but when we in a relationship I don't look at us as a train. Yet it sounds strange and even I don't understand but I look at the situation different.

It was also a fantasy though. I mean watching all those nasty channels I seen the trains and I thought it was unique so whenever you have the chance to carry out your dreams that's awesome. This dream was better in real life though. Pictures in your head of what you saw then being able to try it. Don't judge me try it lol. I will say this though, we both had respect for her, and she had and still have respect for us. At the end of the day this is what it comes to.

Now a days my sex fetish has changed. My preferred things were me, my homie and a female, train as y'all say and now it's me and 2 females. Oh, my goodness it's the best thing in life. So, I had the opportunity to have that back in my younger days, but it just wasn't what it is now.

Back then I was in a house with two female cousins and they both liked me. We were all lying in bed watching a movie and one started to rub my arm then she begun to rub my chest and then she went in my pants! Oh boy I was living. The other started but when she reached in my pants, she felt her cousin hand there and immediately pulled back. Since then, I've been dealing with the cousin who entered first but could never get the other. She was upset that I

10th Ward Buck
entertained the other.

So, years later the opportunity presented itself again. It was me, my fake gf, and what I mean by fake is we had the people thinking we was in a relationship, but it was just a sex thing. Ok, so it was me, her, and then she had friends come over now mind you I was blind not knowing my fake girlfriend liked girls and that her friends were the ones she was having sex with. I was green and blind to it all.

Come to find out later that they wanted to have sex with each other but wanted a male and I was that lucky male that night. So, they in there just talking and drinking and my fake gf told one of the girls; bitch let me touch that pussy. Now first let me say it was me and 3 of them that night. Now me green to the situation, I'm thinking they drunk and just joking but why she really pulled her cloths down and let her rub her private part. Oh boy what was they trying to do me? Lol so then the next thing happened, they started kissing now by this time I'm lost. So, my fake gf told me to come to the top of the bed and waved the other girl to come up. She took girl 3 hand and put it by my private area. Ooooooo myyyyyyy, I was like here we gooo. Then all 3 got completely undressed.

My fake gf then bent over, faced me and pulled my pants down. She began to give me knowledge as the other girl gave her some and girl 3 was behind girl 2. It went down without my permission. However, I'm not complaining then we just went into all kinds of extra activities. She exposed me to something new and spoiled me. After it was all done, I was like am I dreaming.

The next day I had all kinds of questions, but she summed it all up by saying yes. She like girls too and then proceeded to say, "and you can have some of them". Man, I was like girl where you been all my life.

The very next time she got a girl who was a crush of mine on IG. Bruh this was unbelievable, she was making it happen was unbelievable. So, my fake gf was like Buck I got this bitch and she fine, she wants me to come by her, but I don't want her by myself. So, she was like you want to see her and I was like hack yeah. She showed me who she was, and I was like girl you are lying.

In my head I was like I been wanted her. So, she invited her over. When the girl got there, she liked me as well but was playing dumb to my fake gf because she didn't want her to know she liked me.

When they got started, my IG crush told my fake gf that the two can do it, but I can't touch her. Aww it broke my heart but when they started my crush grab me, pulled out my private part, and gave me the yeah with the yeah. It was amazing and once again unbelievable. All my dreams were coming through. I was the luckiest and happiest dude on earth. She later told me I was the perfect person they were looking for due to us all being private about things. She spoiled me and opened me up to a whole new hobby.

The relationship with my fake gf showed me that trust is the main reason people have issues in a relationship. I noticed since we were really together, there was no need for us to build trust when it came to mess with other people, so we didn't fuss like others in a normal relationship.

When trust is an issue things get more serious. For me, because of my past relationships my trust is low. This lil relationship I found myself happier because I felt free. When you with someone and you have to adjust to them and their way of living and their way of doing things you feel boxed in. It's not a good feeling. You want to be with someone who you can feel free around, not free as in cheating or talking to others but free to be happy and talk about things. When you have trust issues then conversations are limited.

You want to share things with the person you in a relationship with but you not sure if they can handle your secrets or use them against you. Your word and trust build relationships and without those, you have nothing. If I can believe your word, then I can't trust you. If I don't trust you then there's no reason for us to be in a relationship. I've noticed that when I don't trust them the interest of me to them gets low. When I don't trust you then I don't believe you. I may listen but that's it.

People try and fast talk you with a lie often. When I hear fast talking that's a green light for me to go and investigate. I play things back in my mind and ask questions before I move on things now. Once a person figure they have you wrapped around their finger then they will tell you the moon pink knowing you would believe it. There are people in relationships who see no wrong in who telling them nothing but lies.

I can't throw names, but I know a female whose been lied to for years. She will overlook the lies for the young man's attention. No matter who he talks to or conversate with she there for him no matter what as long as he gives her time. Like how many times are you going to bump your head for him?

It's hard for me to believe things that are true these days. Lies do something to you. We all know a person who is just a compulsive liar and when that person speaks, we just automatically think they're lying. I want to be in a relationship, but my lack of trust keeps me doubting every female I meet.

I noticed that about me. When a female say she didn't answer or text me back cause of a certain reason I automatically think she is lying. She can be telling the truth but not to me. All I hear is lies. Lies was all I heard in my previous relationship, so it's programmed in my head to tune it out.

A successful relationship has trust. No matter who says what, work on your trust. As I stated your word is all you have, so give your partner that and stand by it. Once trust is broken it's hard to get it back. Especially if it's a lie about you cheating. What we must realize is what we stand to lose if we get caught cheating. Now if your relationship isn't worth anything then step out. Now, if it's who you want to be with them you better tighten up and go with the flow and not a flow that's going to get you caught up. You can apologize after cheating but know what you did don't just go away. Also be mindful that it's going to take a lot to gain that trust and a lot of time.

So, before you step out, know that your word is on the line and that trust level will get low. Both will affect your relationship.

For me, being single sucks. When I'm in a relationship everybody wants me, but when I'm single its crickets or it's a female saying you still in love with your BM. That right there gets me all the time because when I'm with her they be fine with it.

This is the down side of Social Media. The fact that everybody sees your relationship status. When you breakup they assume that person will be are still is in your life. They then move slow on you not realizing you need them to help you get over that person. If you talk to me, give me time and good conversation then that's helping me towards rehabilitation. If I'm not talking to anyone then I'm going to be reaching back out, not always to be back in a relationship but conversation and that be the reason people be back together sometimes.

The plus of being single is that you can talk to who you want to when you want to and how many you want to. For me that's too much. I don't like talking to a lot of people. I don't have that much time in a day. When I do go somewhere with my ex, people assume we together and most of my female friends fall back off me. The minus of being single is you be lonely at night lol. I hate it. I'm used to being laid up and wrapped up. Even if I'm not lonely if you not my woman then I'm not comfortable sleeping with you. I be quick to help pack their things. Not to be rude but if she not mine I want to be free, that way I can talk to others as well. If she still at my house laid up… in respects to her I can't talk to other people. And I'm jealous so I damn sure don't want her texting or calling no dude around me.

I'm the type that just want one person and be great! No, I'm not perfect and yes, I've cheated, but I'll never leave home. It doesn't make sense to cheat but hey it's only lust. I'm saying its only lust, but I be fired up when it happens to me which brings me to my next subject which is being fair.

Fairness in a relationship must happen. You can't do something and not allow to do it. I'm not talking about cheating or anything, but if you go out with your friend or friends you can't look down on it or get mad. I've seen it all too often and have been a part of it.

In one of my relationship my girl went out but when I go out it's so many reasons she gives while I'm out. She be like "you are going out because I went out, you are going for them hoes, you are going out trying to be down with your friend because you don't even go out". Like bruh, no matter what you think if I'm going out let me go out and not be upset about it.

There are so many other examples, but I use this one cause it's at the top when I think about be fair. It is like if you can dish it you should be able to take it and that's where the mix up come in at. People always want to do something to you or say something but don't want it to

10ᵗʰ Ward Buck

happen to them. That's why I relate that to be fair. It's ok to ask not to do a certain thing or ask not to go out but don't demand it. Relationships needs freedom and me time.

To make it last you have to be able to appreciate the togetherness. All that being around each other 24/7 just isn't it. You need room to breathe. Look Bae, you go do that and I am going to do this, and I'll see you later. Now, when we hook back up, we appreciate it more rather than being all up other each like Siamese twins. Communication is key. Talk more, open more and get that understanding that will keep the spark in your relationship.

Chapter 9

I was asked if I ever had a real woman before. The answer to that is yes. I want to say her name but let's call her License Plate LP for short. In respect for her and her current situation.

But when I look back at all my relationships no one came close to the support LP gave me. The cause of our split was me. I was insecure and still at the time not only mentioning BM #1 but was always running behind her.

I met LP at a Halloween party at a club in 2012. I love Halloween parties just to see the girls costumes. The cats and bunnies and police officers… bruh that party be the best.

So, I was paid to perform at the club, I walked in and scanned the crowd as always and for some reason my scanned kept picking this black cat suit with a lil black tail. I couldn't get my eyes off her. I walked closer to get a better view and was like dam and she pretty. She had the lil cat whiskers in her face with the lil black painted nose. I feel in love instantly. I was scared to talk to her. First because of rejection but also because I wasn't sure if she had a man or not and if he was in there. Luckily for me the girl who was with her knew me and noticed me eyeing her and said Buck you must want my friend and I was like yessssss!! She didn't tell her, but I gave her that look like girl I want you.

So, the friend was like I am going to hook you up Buck! I was like yeah do that. She did it and I was in.

At the time I was living in my Restaurant Finger Lickn Wings cause me and #1 just split and moved out the house we were living in.

LP and I clicked quickly, we started going places and seeing each other. It took me some time to take her to the place where I was living because it wasn't a house but talking to her about my situation and opening up with the truth made her be like that's that I'm not judging you I'm down.

So, we went to my place and she ended up staying the night and came often after that. I was like if she accepted this then I know she's the one.

When I had events, she was there in full support. Don't have a problem wearing my gear and most importantly she would advertise my events without me having to ask. LP was the one.

I speak about a lot of women not knowing what the right man looks like. Well I took her for granted not knowing what the right woman looks like.

Because of my fresh breakup I wouldn't trust her. Every time she went somewhere, I would question that. I would question when she doesn't answer my calls, text etc. I just became a complete monster and to add some truth it's not only causes of what's has been done to me in my past, but I was cheating. The fact that I was doing me on the side had me thinking she was doing her. I had no chill when it came to accuse her of things.

As I look back, I'm realizing that I was too hard on her. My actions towards her made me a ticking time bomb and I exploded and ran her away. I didn't see my aggression at first. I also saw how people especially women are scared when they are done a certain thing.

You cannot do things to people and not expect consequences. I was wrong, I mean if I was going to do me, I should have just taken my lick if she was doing something and at least till I seen it myself.

Now she's been put in my shoes cause when I was in my first relationship people would always tell number 1, I'm doing this and that, but she couldn't verify that. Her friends were jealous of what I was doing for her and the fact I stopped a lot of that foolishness she was doing especially going out constantly. So, when I thought of accusing LP of cheating, I should have thought about the times when I was being accused of things.

When you are in a relationship the support of your mate is important. If nobody else, you need that extra help from your mate. I noticed my more successful times was either when I'm single or when I was in a relationship with LP. When I'm by myself I focus on me. I can do everything I need for me ensuring I'm straight. All time, energy and money dedicated to me.

10th Ward Buck

Before my first BM I was the shit. I slowed down made it about her and lost contact with my fan base. After her it shot back up. Then I met LP and it got better. When it comes to support of your mate, she was the definition of it. She would post my events on her social media. She would spread the word and even invite her family and friends. Not one, I mean not one, none of my relationships had the full commitment like the one with LP.

In my past relationships I've put my all into the females weather it was a business or just making them look good or making them a name. In doing so they didn't know the role they had to play to keep me relevant. Instead of them telling people about my businesses and things I had going on, they didn't and if they did it was last minute or because I got upset with them from not understanding that that's their job as my girlfriend.

Just like with children when we tell them it starts at home, same applies when it comes to relationship support. You can't be in a relationship with a person and feel you don't need to help them. Even if it seems they have it offer help.

Y'all be wanting the finer things in life but don't want to work for them. Yes work! Most of y'all rather look for someone who have it already then to work and help your own man or woman. Free loaders are what I call them. Want to jump on the bus but wouldn't help change the tire if it was to get flat. I miss that support from LP. You know they say you don't miss good things until they're gone. Well that's true.

When I see couples like Jay Z and Beyoncé, I feel some type of way because I'm like how the hell I don't have that kind of support. All this money and time I'm putting in their ass and they can't do the simple shit. LP didn't ask me for a dime in fact she had a job and was consistent and didn't allow this social media stuff to get to her. She was well mannered and represented me well. She wasn't a fool though, she didn't let who I am get the best of her. If she had to speak her mind about something, she did it. She didn't let me slide with nothing. She really cared unlike others that had that I don't give a fuck attitude. Those are the people you want to stay away from cause if they don't care they really don't care.

If you win, they in if you lose it isn't their fault. All they want is the best from them and no one else. They don't understand it takes team work. If you want to live this life you living as far as being self-employed and single you have to work, put in your time to help. It's all on me though because people will only do what you allow.

I've been allowing a lot just because I wanted them happy and that's why they never worried about helping or understood the importance of their help. One day I'll find me another LP cause that's all I need and I'm going get that million-dollar check. I'm not saying I need someone but it's nice to have one. Especially a down chick.

With all my current success I think if I was with LP as of now, I'll be further. The reason I say that is cause after our split I went backwards. I stopped giving events, I stopped doing music and I slowed down on my Instagram. I was all over the place but wasn't nowhere if you know what I mean. All this could have been avoided if I just tune my insecurity down. It's going be hard but I'm going to try my best when I get in my next relationship.

LP was fun, loving and caring. I didn't have that in none of my relationship. We used to talk, joke and play. These are things I missed. These are needed in a relationship. I'm not sure what the hell I was tripping off, but I was tripping. I had what I needed in front of me but still wanted to play around. My ex wrecked my car, so I was getting around in rentals.

LP and I found a place to finance so she got both our cars in her name. That was a big help. She also appreciates what I did for her. If she didn't like the gift or whatever she didn't show it. She would smile making me feel like I'm the best man on earth. I must note I am the best when it comes to giving, surprises and making my girl look good. Unlike my other relationships', LP didn't have messy friends, or shall I say mess when it came to me and telling her things about me.

I was amazed by that cause all my other relationships my gfs had friends that was just disgusting. They would control her as far as telling her things and making he believe them. Social media is my thing but all of a sudden, my ex friends front and center taking badly about me. I'm like wait, if you have a problem with me tell me why you are telling the world.

I then noticed they was looking for attention. They say they don't but If you didn't you wouldn't be on the internet explaining your fake dislike for me. My only downfall is the women I chose. As long as I'm single and don't have no one talking down on me. I'm good but the moment an ex gets on social media and rant people believe them.

Dudes dislike me because they either had past dealings with an ex of mine or they wanted them. So, when a dude gets a chance to confront my ex, they go to talking bad about me just to become their friend.

For years the gay factor has been chasing me. I'm not gay but I see it's a way to make me look bad and get the females not to deal with me. Dudes funny and cut throat when it comes to females. I never had personal beef. Ask around nobody could say they have a personal problem with me, if they do it's pertaining to one of my ex. These dudes would come out nowhere and be all in her dm.

For me I be like damn you used to talk to him, him, him and him. I swear I be drove because I don't be knowing those dudes until my ex gets caught up with one of them. Crazy is they all know me. That's embarrassing to have a female with you but when she in the club with a million dudes run up or secretly speaks to her. That's an all-around female and I have a habit of choosing the same type. Now I see you can't just look for looks you also have to look for brains. Y'all out there saying y'all want this one and that one but they out there looking good but can't spell the basic shit.

I don't want them anymore. Now you must match my energy and situation because I need someone compatible to me. I need one woman. One who kicks into action when it's time to get to the business. I don't want no freeloaders. In the word relationship there's relate and so in order to be together and to be on the same page you have to relate to each other. You won't agree and relate on everything but the closer you are the better. When you first meet someone is the time you should be evaluating. Check them out, see if it's worth your time and listen. They tell you all before you go with your next move. Get the understanding you need and watch how things take off.

I don't just go out looking for a female but when I do see one, I look for that lil slim thing lol. People always say you need a woman and you choosing wrong. Well it's not like I'm on a dating contest. When I see someone, and we click only time will tell if that person is down or not. It's hard to tell who is who in the beginning.

I would admit I've chosen some childish females but hey, who knew? A few of the girls I've chosen not known to me was popular in their communities. I'll have different people saying don't mess with her she's such and such, but I don't judge off what I hear, and I've heard a lot.

Reason I don't listen to what people say is people say a lot about me too and I know it is lies. With that being said I listen but that don't stop my approach especially if I like what I see. I'm laughing because people act like I'm supposed to give the girls a quiz before I converse with them. My problems are I feel like I don't need the girls to do anything, so I don't expect anything from them, and they get used to it.

On the other hand, I expect them to know that when I need help to join it. This is the part that makes me upset with them. I'll be working on a certain project and as I'm working, they wouldn't offer any help. It breaks me down. My relationships went haywire majority of the times because of me fussing about their lack of help. What get me the most is when I'm working, and they come fucking with me with bs. I be like so you are going to be doing this all day, this all you do. Or when they doubt me saying isn't nobody going to that cause everybody going be over at another spot. I be like I know this slow Mf didn't just say that and then boom I explode.

If you don't believe, then just keep your comments to yourself if you trying to motivate me the wrong way. How you are going make me go against what I feel is right for me. They already don't try to help but want to add salt to injury by saying all that stupid shit. Women knows how to get under a man skin.

Boy there isn't anything like when I give an event and my gf would be at another, like wtf! You got to be kidding me. The icing on the cake is when her friend or friends discuss an event and she be all for it.

As I look back, I see the signs of immaturity. I can't believe the things that was said while I was trying to put things together. There is y'all case about needing a woman but even with a woman I need someone committed.

10th Ward Buck

Commitment is the key to all this. Once you commit to me you are all into any and everything I do.

Just using my own life experience, I saw where my gf would support total strangers before supporting me. It's crazy how that shit happens but it's what I allowed and what I let them get used to. Instead of me paying other people we can keep the money in our household. Before they see it like that, they'll holla you better pay somebody to do it. Once the money stops the relationship stops. Believe this. If I'm taking care of them it's all good but the moment, I say no then I'm the baddest person on earth to them. Talking about I never do nothing and the things I did do I was supposed, and I be like well damn I did do shit. At that point everything I've done goes out the window. She would make a statement "like all that stuff you did was old, and I didn't need nothing you brought you did that cause you wanted to". The one that really ticked me off is when she said I could've got that for myself. Boy boy boy ungrateful and selfishness at its best.

This is how and why I started to bring things to social media because I wanted to share my story and vent. This way helped me instead of having all that bottled in and what I've found out is that others were going through the same shit. So y'all judge me on my life it's just the only difference my life is public but best believe, I'm not the only one going through bs in a crappy relationship.

Sometimes the person we want isn't the person we need. Relationship, friendships and even kinships get toxic. You have to know when to leave. I don't believe in going from person to person or relationship to relationship so that's why I get caught up in loving hard. In the mix of me loving hard I find it hard letting go of people even though I've caught them cheating or even lie in to me. I give chances more than the norm. I rather work things out then to be apart.

I'm a family person so I do my best to keep us together especially since I have kids. I hate for my kids to be raised in a broken home, but I've realized that I rather toxic thus go and live a healthier life then to be in a home where these fussing or even less communication between their parents. My kids are at the age where they soak things up. They also go to school with other kids who see my social media, or their parents are following me. Knowing this I toned down the entertainment on some of the things I was doing.

Once my son was teased by a student that attended his school said that his mother said I was gay. That caused a problem as my son came into my defense arguing with the student leading to a fight and suspension from school. One thing I tell my kids is don't worry about what others say. I explained to them who I am and the affect I have on people. I let them know people have no reason to dislike me, but we can't make everybody like me, and everybody won't like me, and just like me everybody won't like them.

However, I also told them the love will outweigh the hate. Don't focus on who don't like you and don't acknowledge it or them. A fire will get wilder when gasoline is poured on it. Any bad situation, I make it as a fire and be the water to it and ignore it and it will go away.

10th Ward Buck

So as much as I wanted to be with their mother, she wasn't the one. I wanted her but she wasn't the one to get us to the next level. Next level is owning our own home etc. If you with someone and they're not helping you excel then you are with the wrong person. Looks goes out the window if you can't advance with that person. Most of us have talent but don't go forward because we are looking for help in our relationship and we not getting it, so we give up. I've done my own research on me and I found my relationship was my hold up.

As I said before I allowed them to do everything except support me. Fuck sex, fuck looks fuck it all if you don't have support from them. Not to exclude fuck your money yep fuck their money if they don't support you. Some people will use their money to control you. I don't want that I want us both to have freedom and feel free. Don't eat my fish come fish with me so you can have your own. Don't spend time under someone and don't learn or do things for your own independence. You up there all under someone for what they have and the moment they leave you have nothing. Not only will you have nothing you won't know how to do nothing. I'm in the mode where I'm now looking for what I need over what I want cause from my experience. What I want haven't been good for me. It's like being lactose intolerant and still drink milk. Now I'm learning from my past. Before I didn't but that's the best part of life. Learning from experience and learning from mistakes. Even though you love or want someone it doesn't mean that they are the one.

Chapter 10

Before I got in a relationship with #1, I was popular and well liked with no hate. When we started dating, I started to get disliked by dudes who either was talking to her before me or dudes that wanted her. I never knew these dudes even existed until her. The crazy thing is I always new someone who knew one of the dudes. I was in my own Lil world, so I wasn't worried about who was popping in whatever part of town they were in because I was in my own Lil space.

At first, I couldn't understand it but started to show that it wasn't me but her entertaining these dudes. It would be so many occasions where she'll see a certain dude speak and make me think it was a cousin or one of her friend's boy.

Now me I am not new to it all, so whatever she told me I believed. Then it started to get worst cause the girls in my hood would mess with some of the same dudes or their friends. They would come to me and be like Buck you know your girl was with such and such or she was in the car with such and such. Then boom I pulled up and witnessed it for myself and this is the moment that turned me into a monster. As far as what I would post on social media about her.

The things that I posted about her were the things that made people turn on me and started to dislike me. I'm not that person to do those things but I was embarrassed and hurt. As a man especially me because I love hard. There was no outlet for me to vent so I vented on social media and the reason I vented there because this is the same place, I put her on a high pedestal making her look like the queen of the city. I'm up there bragging and this and that and all awhile she is cheating. Boy was I fired up.

I would upload our messages, pictures, videos you name it I was insane. The things I was doing cause people to be like no man not going to do this to their baby momma.

What I didn't understand about that is a woman can do it with no consequences but the moment a man do it he a punk! Well with me I gave her a look that I assumed was good, but she gave me a look as a duck. I'm doing all this for her, and she is playing me. I was stressed, trying to understand it. Even though the posting was looked down on cause I'm a man I felt as if some things needs to be addressed and I did that. I don't think she should get away with things and I get the blamed for my wrong doing.

Yes, I know 2 wrongs don't make a right but at that moment I was like fuck all that I was heated. People have done worst when they caught their partner cheating so that lil posting wasn't really shit it just gave people a reason to be vocal against me.

Before that happened, they had no reason to talk about me, leading me to believe they been jealous. Had I not posted the things I posted on social about her I wouldn't be New Orleans most hated. However, with me I know there's more love for me than hate so I used the hate as a footstool. Anytime I had a chance to I capitalized off anything a person tried to do to take me down. If I had the chance to erase those post and not do it, I wouldn't because of the way the world set up.

The reason of me posting those things was to bring awareness to this cheating shit but it back fires as even though she was wrong. There were so many taking her side and even saying I'm glad you cheated on him. Truthfully saying even though I got backlash about it when I did do it and vented, I felt great. Ironically, I felt so good because when I post or talk about my life, I want people to learn and not have to go through the same shit I did. My life is public so I give the public things that I think they should know.

From being a monster to doing shit in a movie. So, we back home working on us. Everything seemed fine. I started to work on my new business Finger Lickn Wings and at this point I started to really notice I was getting no support from this girl. Everybody was excited about the new business especially since it's in the hood where I'm from. I took an old run-down cleaner on the corner of Jackson Avenue and Annunciation St and made it a restaurant making that corner no longer an eye soar.

I'll be at home with a few friends and family doing taste test and all kind of other things pertaining to the restaurant and #1 never showed interest. I then became vocal about it and she'll be like here you go I thought we was working on us and me wanting it to work I was like you right plus I was too excited to even keep the argument going. So, I was like ok.

The crazy thing is she didn't do not 1 thing to help me with my restaurant not 1 but as soon as I had the grand opening there, she was floating through the doors like Michelle Obama or something. It goes to show you that people would show up at your celebration but wouldn't help you promote it. I preach this all the time, they will not be there during the struggle but all over you when the success hits.

The next day after the opening I stayed home to work on the pace of the restaurant, that same day she said she had to go to a card game. I believed her cause she was in a club where in order for people to attend your card game you have to attend theirs. If you don't go to the game, you had to pay them and there were serval times where she had to pay, and it came out my pockets.

Sometimes I had a show, or we'll be out of town somewhere. We'll this day I got a phone call that she was in the east whereas the card game was supposed to be uptown. Now if she went to the card game or not. I don't know but I do know the game was over and when I called for her, she would pick up and hang up. Somehow my cousin knew where she was not the exact house but the street.

So, I'm calling and calling no answer no as I'm in route to the area where she at. We get to the street and my cousin noticed the car, what car? The same car I bought her in the previous month. Not knowing who house or what can happen we started knocking on the door and ringing the doorbell. A lady comes to the door, we asked for #1 and the lady said she not there.

10th Ward Buck

As we are leaving, we heard something in the back yard and as we got closer, we heard mourning, sex mourning! I pushed the gate and there she was outside in the backyard having sex! They both ran into the house. As I was leaving the lady came back and said she is here, but I didn't know so they must have gone straight to the back yard.

When I saw that I could've passed out. Boy I didn't know if I was coming or going. At this time on my way home everything started to make sense. Why she didn't support, why she didn't come around and why she was at so many card games. All to get away and be with him. The same dude she just got busted with and cried like she was going to change.

Y'all have no idea how heartbreaking that is. Not just to catch her cheating but having sex, then outside. So, she didn't come home for a few days, but I wasn't going to let that slide so she called talking bout she misses me. I was like no you don't miss me, you just don't have nowhere to stay but I played it cool cause I wanted to play catch back.

By then though she was talking to another dude and I'm finding this out too, so she was lying and all that. She came back home I couldn't just let her in, so I had to Yike her real quick.

Fast forward one day she lied about going to a friend sleep over but come to find out she was by the other dude house. She called me the next day not knowing I had all the info on her. Even heard the dude bragging and that's the part I hate. Dudes don't say they fucked this one and that one they say I fucked 10th Ward Buck girl. Bruh I hate the fuck out that shit because it be the same dudes talking about, I'm gay but want to get a rep off my name come on bruh. What make the rep worst is that the girls I messed with allow them to do the shit.

Anyways one day I got news on where she was because was lying. This time it was a friend who not only told me where she was but told me where she went. Oh boy, so me and my potner E plotted up to go get her.

Before I left, I put black pepper in my hand, you know I don't want to fight her, so I put the pepper in my hand and asked E to drive. When I pulled up, I was nice and calm, and she came down. After her friend thought it was ok, she went inside.

We then focused on her in the car then I began to question her and asked about the backyard sex again and the new sleep over situation, she wouldn't admit so I took the pepper and threw it in her face. I was out of it, lost and confused you name it. All this time I'm focused on family, her and my business, but I was green to the sneaky shit she was doing.

Bruh I was blind to it all then it's like the bs couldn't stop. I'm hearing about this and that. I'm like well dam if you messing with all these dudes where is the money? Cause you sure don't have none and anything you do have comes from me but then boom. It was told she was having sex for Jordan's or card game money. And it made sense because it was always around that time when Jordan's was released, and she'll lose the money I give her and end being at the card games the next day. I used to think she was winning at the card games and buying her own Jordan's but no Mr. Buck you've been sold a dream. This just took me by surprise and dropped my trust level so low. I wouldn't wish this on nobody.

Luckily for me I had social media to vent out to and as I said they may dislike me for doing so but I didn't kill anyone. You have people that can't take all that and that's a lot. As I'm thinking and writing I see I been through some shit.

I've concluded that monsters are created in people because you can be the sweetest but so many problems throwed at you eventually you will breakdown. People hold me to a high standard, and I don't want that. I don't want to be judged. I want to be regular just like everyone else and be able to make mistakes without being judged. My situation isn't any different then another person who's going through it.

I feel as though sense I have a name people say they expect that from me, ha ha hell I bleed and cry just like everybody else. And everything she did to me caught up and broke me down because it wasn't like I caught a lil here and a Lil there it all came at once like a hurricane. Like hurricane Katrina I was not ready nor prepared for it.

What kept me going strong was my momma. She wouldn't tell me leave or stay but to do what's right for me.

Since I wanted her and wanted a family, I thought what was right for me. I was keeping her even with all this bad baggage but for me I was blinded by the fact that I was in love and maybe she had love for me but there was no connection between us and without that there's no relationship and that's why she stepped out so many times. I'm a business man, that's too boring for her nor was it was her thing. She wanted more and she wanted to be able to relate to her friends so what I was doing in their eyes was lame. He is being a person who's easily influenced got influenced and became a cheater and an often one.

The next situation turned me from doing shit in a movie to finally being physical. At this time, we were living in River Garden aka the 10th Ward formally known as the St. Thomas projects. It was me, her, our 2 kids, my brother and our friend. I was in the mix of trying to make things right with her after the internet rant and it seemed as if she was trying to be more committed to me.

So, I was like you know what it's time for a new car so I went and got her a brand new all white Benz, it was clean too. I kept it at the lot until night, so she won't see it cause I wanted to surprise her. I went about 5pm before they closed and parked it near the house. I asked my friend to ride with me when she went to sleep so I can park it in front the house so she can see it.

Once we got to the house he asked if he can see the car to go out! Jokingly, but me as a friend was like hey go head, I wanted him to show it off.

10th Ward Buck

Woke up the next morning excited to show her, walked outside then boom the car was totaled, wrecked to the frame! What's worst is I didn't get the full coverage insurance because I had to get it switched to mine the next day when they opened. I got just enough coverage from the dealership to get it home. I was fired up! I went upstairs and I was like bruh, what happened? He first was acting sleepy then started to act drunk then he said he wasn't in the car.

I was standing there like I know this dude not lying in my face. I'm heated and started to explain to her what the fuck happened. I asked to use my girl phone to call the police to get a police report and in the call log there was his number several times, but I didn't make nothing of it.

After calling the police and then the dealership luckily for me I had a friend who worked there. She made the insurance policy active. But I was still out of my $3500 down payment and the $550 insurance payment.

Later down the road I get into her Instagram to find out she was having sex with another dude. Bruh, I couldn't believe the messages and how personal they were. It wasn't too detailed about sex, but you knew it was just from reading. I had to ask first so I went and picked her up. I made her feel comfortable as if I didn't know then I asked her. Of course, she started to lie then I showed her, and she just admitted to having sex with him.

I was shocked! especially to find out that the person was the same person who wrecked her car! Yes, my so-called friend. A friend who was living with us. He's been living with us for about 2 years, so all kinds of shit were playing in my head. It didn't help me one-bit I started to fight her. She never seen this before, so she was like Buck Buck what are you doing! My response was beating your ass!

I can't believe you was fucking my friend and a friend who was living not staying but living with us. I know y'all are like what I did the friend well at this time he been gone about a month due to the car situation had us nothing really speaking.

As far as her, she went pillow to post for about a month. She would call and I'll ignore. This was just the most. Of all things my friend? Come on nah. I went to my momma and told her what's happening, and I was crying as my momma talked. At the end of her talk she said son, no matter who you are you are not excluded from this like this, this can happen to anyone. From that moment, I instantly stopped crying. That there was deep! I was like I'm 10th Ward Buck, I got this going on and that I shouldn't be cheated on, but my mother summed it up. Anything can happen to anybody.

With all this that number 1 did me… I know y'all like why you still put up with her!? Well, not only was it the kids and wanting to be a family but I was whipped. Seriously, I was sex whipped. I mean the girl put it on me like no other. Even when I cheated or tried to play catch back. I haven't met a female yet to have sex like her. Now y'all may be saying there's more to life than sex, yes that's true but sex is a part of life. Being that I be so busy, whenever I can get it, I cherish it lol. I can go on about how good she does it but all I'm going to say is think of your best times!

That's why still to this day we were still having sex and going through our Lil ups and downs like we were in a relationship together because we were still having sex. The reason anytime she needed me I was there. No matter who I was talking to or in a relationship with I was going to get me some of #1!

The whole city and my followers were like what the hell is she doing to him that he just keeps going back after she do such and such to him, well there you have it. I did what I had to even going the extra mile fake crying in court with my kids to keep her from being locked up. When she did get locked up oh boy, I was like oh no.

So, one place I can see her, but I was on the other side of the glass. I asked her to slide her pants down so I can see it. At first, she was scared but once we got used to it for them lil 3 months. I couldn't wait until visitation day. Lol boy when I tell you it was like a private show.

By this time, I'm convinced that I'm just hooked on it. I'm sorry older people and my church people who are reading I just had to let this truth off my chest because I've done a lot and got done a lot and this is the reason why!

So, they shipped her off. Now I had to ride an hour to see her. First 2 times was with the kids but then I noticed I can get close and touch her. Oooooo weeee! You don't miss things until it's gone, lmao!

The next trip I didn't bring the kids cause I had a plan. I wanted to touch her and it and get a kiss and as planned it happened. All smiles going back home, and the trip started to seem shorter.

Here it is the last run of me being sneaky. The phone watch came out, so I was able to get it in but on the way out they caught me with it. All man I had all my lil butt shots and stuff but good thing the watch was locked. The guards tried to get in and they couldn't I told them it's broken that I just wear it for show. They said if I bring something like that again I'll be banned. All man there goes my Lil show.

Although my lil pictures didn't make it home the lil trips to see her was awesome and fun and before you know it, she was home. I know most of y'all wonder what she's in jail for. It was shop lifting.

Now when we were together, she didn't do that or at least to my knowledge. So, when it was brought to me, I was shocked! Then it would go from wanted papers to the news. Oh boy, I was lost and embarrassed. Even though we weren't together people paired us. Some started saying I taught her, I influenced her, and I knew she was a shoplifter. All those or false. I don't condone that. It had me looking bad.

No matter what she did me and who she was talking to, I made it my duty to let her know about herself, that it was wrong, and I also defended her. All the good I do and was doing for her went unnoticed but when it was bad it seems like everybody it's downing me. The support I gave her. The only one in court daily, the only one who made every visitation, the one who accepted every call. All this went out the window and what made it worst some people went to praising the people who left her high and dry. Me and number 1 been through it all even a tv show. When it was all said and done, I was stuck with the kids. I called up this talk show called The Test and they flew us in, and we made the show. That day the whole city was amped about it. People was leaving work early, getting their kids from school early you name it the city wasn't missing that show. It had its serious moments but in all it was fun and entertaining. In all I love number 1 and my actions showed, and the hard love got me cheated on driving me to post about her on Social media allowing people to judge me the wrong way.

I'm nothing of what they make me out to be. The cheating pushed me and embarrassed me to a point of not wanting to fight or anything. I then took it to social media, and therefore I have a bad rap and a picture of me so blurry because they see the good but they trying to understand the bad but how can I be bad but so good. I've blocked so many people from voicing their opinion until they became a hate Buck social aid and pleasure club. I have more love than hate and that's a fact it just a hand full who dis like me cause of my own life. That is crazy. I haven't done any of them nothing personally.

How and why would you dis like me anyway when I give you entertainment, been for years. I give y'all music and I give y'all events. I keep you all tuned in and I find things to talk about so your day at home or work can fly by. I need y'all to look back at my life, my story and see what I say vs what was said, and you'll see the truth is here and I didn't cut no corners.

I finally can move forward with getting all this off my chest because I can admit I was a fool for love. Not too many can do so and not too many will admit they was a sucker for love. She tore me down but I'm going to blame myself. Me wanting the best for her and loving hard got me looked at different by the people because my payback was venting on social media. I've learned my lesson in the fact that you can't share everything with everybody and that everybody isn't for you.

Who is 10th Ward Buck? I'm a man, a father, a son, a brother a friend, a relative, entertainer and a God-fearing man. I want the best for all and wising success for all who shoot for it. I have no ill will for none of Gods' people. No beef and can't no one say I disrespected them or told them anything out of line. Ask around, all bad you'll hear is what I've posted on social media other than that my life, my music and my entertainment is all in line for the good. This is the reason I can't be phased by the hate and lies. I am born Marlon Justin Horton known to the world as 10th Ward Buck and my words to you is get to know me before you allow others to Judge me for you. God Bless!

10th Ward Buck

www.ingramcontent.com/pod-product-compliance
Lightning Source LLC
Chambersburg PA
CBHW060343100426
42812CB00003B/1102